Xenia Field's Gardening Week by Week

TREASURE PRESS

Foreword

This is not an arbitrary or legally binding Book of Rules.

My book gives friendly advice as to how the many garden chores of the year can or might be fairly evenly spread over the weeks.

Much will depend on the size of the garden (and the gardener), the time available, and the kind of weather we have.

Some, but not all the jobs will get done, but enough of them, I hope, to give you a generous return in flowers, vegetables and fruit.

Xenia Field

Contents

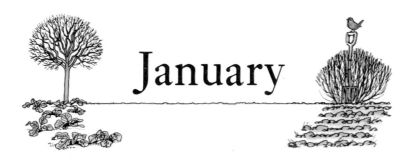

January

This is usually the coldest month of the year. Conditions are frustrating to the gardener with many left-over jobs from December waiting to be done.

If new plants arrive when the ground is frozen or very wet, heel them in temporarily in a 'warm' corner of the garden or put them in a frost-proof shed while the cold spell lasts, but they must be kept moist.

Small plants and roses can be brought into the house, undone and the roots covered with damp sacking.

Cultivators, mowers, shears and all tools in need of sharpening should be serviced without further delay.

All seats and other garden furniture brought under cover in early winter should now be cleaned and treated with preservatives.

Gardeners with a pool and responsibility for goldfish should take precautions against thick ice forming by keeping handy a rush mat, board or even tennis balls to place in the water when severe weather is forecast. Do not break ice with a heavy instrument and cause concussion.

Birds with their ever-changing and growing tastes for forsythia, wisteria, currants, polyanthus, crocus and what-have-you, are a menace.

There are sprays that keep the birds off but they are often washed away with the first shower: there are also dangling what-nots that jangle and are said to frighten the feathered world, but you cannot fool the birds for long. Scaraweb, a spider-like fabric, is probably the best hope of stopping the birds stripping plants of buds.

What were your good resolutions this year? To clean out the bottom of the hedges, weeds, leaves, debris and all? To tidy up the potting shed, wash the pots and crocks and bundle up the stakes? Or weed the lawn?

Whatever your intent, do not forget to examine the begonias, dahlias, gladioli and vegetable roots for damp or rot.

Much time is spent indoors during the next two months, giving the gardener an opportunity of looking after his house plants. Here are a few cultural hints to help keep the plants in good order.

Water with care, not by rota, but when the plant is thirsty (when the soil is pale coloured, the ring of the pot is hollow when you tap it with stick or knuckle, and the pot light when lifted). Beware of over-watering during the winter when the plant is resting, but not even the cactus should be allowed to become desert dry.

The plant must not be left standing in a saucer of water for any length of time.

Give the plant a light position and bring it into the warm side of the curtains on a cold night.

Plenty of fresh air will keep plants healthy.

Keep as even a temperature as possible: plants resent hot days and cold nights. (There should be no more than 8°C. (14°F.) between the two.)

Keep your plant away from all forms of artificial heat. A layer of gravel on a tray or saucer, kept damp, will increase humidity.

Don't over-feed with fertilizer and never feed a plant when dry or ailing. Over-feeding is the beginner's temptation: follow the manufacturer's instructions to the letter; plants dislike all excesses.

The chlorophytum, or spider plant, is indestructible and the perfect beginner's plant.

A cropping plan should be made so that no given group of vegetables is allotted the same land two years running. The rotation of crops reduces the carry-over of pests and diseases. 'The Vegetable Garden Displayed', published by the Royal Horticultural Society, is the most helpful book on this subject, and vegetable growing generally.

Iris unguicularis.

January
Week 1

Garden flowers

Root cuttings of 2–2½ ins. can be taken of anchusa, phlox, Drumstick Primula, *Primula denticulata*, Tree Poppy, *Romneya coulteri*. They should be housed in seed boxes of sandy compost and placed in the greenhouse or cold frame.

Violets in frames will benefit if lights are lifted or removed on mild days.

Plant out the forced bulbs that have flowered and faded. Flower heads should be removed but foliage must be left to die back naturally.

If you feel energetic, start digging the dahlia bed introducing well-rotted manure as you go. The dahlia likes it rich.

Indoor plants

The gift plant: the florist or gift plant is a favourite Christmas or New Year's present. It comes straight from the greenhouse and often finds its new quarters and master unacceptable. Many of the plants die before they have finished flowering. They miss the even temperature, the humidity, and above all the professional gardener and his know-how with the watering can.

There are of course temporary residents that arrive at the peak of their splendour, and once having flowered have no more to give and can be thrown away.

Here are a few tips to keep two popular gift plants in good order.

Azalea indica is usually pot-bound and is therefore madly thirsty. It is one of the few plants that can be safely left with water in its saucer. If placed on a tray of moist pebbles and syringed from time to time it will hold its foliage and last much longer. It will benefit by being taken out of a hot room at night and put in a cooler place out of the draught.

Once flowers have faded the plants should be given to a friend with a greenhouse or when spring comes plunged in the garden for the summer, and brought back in the house before the frost.

Neck and neck in popularity with the azalea comes the poinsettia. This plant should be kept away from artificial heat and the water supply gradually reduced when the coloured bracts fade. Foliage can be cut down and the poinsettia repotted in May using a sandy loam with an addition of peat: after watering it should be plunged outdoors in a sheltered spot until September.

Shrubs

Plant deciduous trees and shrubs in frost-free soil and mulch with peat.

Greenhouse

Top ventilators (away from the prevailing wind) will give all the ventilation that is needed this month.

Dahlias can be started in trays of sandy soil to provide cuttings. (Cuttings of young stock often give the best flowers.)

Chrysanthemums: spray or fumigate with nicotine insecticide or use a malathion aerosol spray.

Cuttings of medium exhibition varieties may be taken from stools throughout the month and set out in boxes in the same way as the dahlias. John Innes Potting Compost No. 1, or equal parts of peat and sand, is a suitable rooting medium. The chrysanthemum enjoys a steady temperature of 10°C. (50°F.).

Make a January sowing in moderate heat of sweet peas for flowering in July and late shows indoors.

Cyclamen should be returned to the greenhouse when showing signs of collapse, through lack of humidity and an indifferent atmosphere. This sad condition can often be avoided by standing the pot on moist pebbles, or better still, dropping the pot into a larger container and filling the margin between the two containers with moss kept constantly moist.

Vegetables

'The early digger gets the best crops' is an old axiom that holds good.

Plant the shallots.

Sow tomatoes, lettuce and onions in gentle heat for early cropping.

Dig, dig, dig to get the soil weathered.

Fruit

Finish spraying. A powerful spray of winter wash will penetrate the hidden crevices of the bark; the ground below the tree should also be treated when possible. The work must be done in the absence of frost and arctic winds.

Viburnum fragrans presents pink apple-blossom flowers from November to March. A twig on the mantelpiece will fill the room with sweet scent.

January
Week 2

Garden flowers

Examine dahlia stems and tubers regularly and dust with sulphur if there is any suspicion of mould.

Sow sweet peas (autumn sowing in pots or peat blocks preferable for early shows). Seeds sown this month will need the moderate warmth of a greenhouse *until* germination takes place.

Some varieties are hard skinned: soak these overnight before sowing and lightly scratch through the skin on the opposite side to the eye before planting.

Michaelmas daisies and similar characters will be found persistent trespassers and must be kept in place. The strong outside growth should be retained and the tired centre discarded later on. If fine spikes are wanted for exhibition, the number of stems allowed to develop from a single root stock must be strictly limited.

A lily of the valley bed can be started in semi-shade, and leafmould will be appreciated.

Have you fed the freesias? They will enjoy a mild liquid feed or a light top-dressing.

Dig on – prepare a bed for the hardy chrysanthemums.

Shrubs

Some mice, not all, have a nasty way of damaging stems of trees and shrubs and can be kept away by rubbing stems with a strong smelling carbolic soap, or bitumen tree dressing.

Mistletoe gets a tremendous boost at Christmas time and gardeners are encouraged to grow it. This semi-parasite grows frequently but not always on the apple tree.

It is important to let the seeds ripen in the berry until late February. A berried bunch may be hung outdoors against a sheltered wall until the seed is ripe, or a berry-bearing twig in a vase of water can be placed in a sunny window to ripen.

Although the apple is the mistletoe's first choice (much will depend on the host from which the berry comes), it will consent to grow on a hawthorn, poplar, lime or oak. A fairly young branch, out of view of the birds, should be chosen, and a cut made in the underside of the branch. The berry should then be pressed into the incision; the sticky pulp should hold the seed in place.

It may take two or three years before the mistletoe grows well. A sheltered position will increase the chance of success.

Trees can sometimes be bought with mistletoe growing on them, but it is more rewarding to grow your own.

Greenhouse

Pot on the autumn-sown sweet peas taking the greatest care not to injure or disturb the delicate root nodes. Place the pots in a cold frame, but wait for a few days before watering the young plants in.

Keep the schizanthus bushy by pinching back the long shoots. Stake the plants early rather than late and treat them to fortnightly doses of weak liquid manure.

Chrysanthemums: prepare a generous supply of rooting compost for cuttings. A mixture of equal parts of peat and sand or John Innes Potting Compost No. 1 is suitable.

Go on taking cuttings of Large Exhibitions until the end of the month keeping the temperature steady at 10°C. (50°F.).

Cuttings of ivies can be taken now and the small variegated ivies make attractive camouflage for the rubber plant that has shed its lower leaves.

Chrysanthemum stools should now be providing cuttings. These should be taken below a leaf joint, dipped in a rooting powder, and kept close in gentle warmth (a polythene bag is helpful if the propagating box is full).

Vegetables

Examine all clamps for decay or mice; a clamp consists of a cone-shaped heap of stored roots covered with a thick layer of straw and beaten down soil.

Warning: liming is useful for keeping roots of the cabbage tribe free of disease, but apt to encourage scab in potatoes.

Herbs

Prepare for a herb garden, if one is not already in existence.

Fruit

Is all pruning finished? Apples and pears can be left until later, but must be pruned while dormant. Cherries can be cut in safety once the sap is rising, when they are more resistant to disease.

General

Fallen leaves, where pests and fungi over-winter, should be collected regularly and burnt.

The Saintpaulia comes from the tropics and enjoys the steady warmth of central heating. Move your plant away from the window on a cold night.

January
Week 3

Garden flowers

Tidy the rockery, and remove all debris and fallen leaves.

Find an inconspicuous corner to plant out the indoor bulbs that have flowered in the house. Turn out the bowls with as little disturbance to roots as possible and leave all foliage intact, but remove dead flower heads.

Top-dress the pinks with lime rubble.

Dahlia stems and tubers should be dusted with sulphur if there is any suspicion of mould.

Sitting in front of the fire in the evening thumbing through the colourful catalogues is an extremely pleasant chore.

The seed catalogues tumble into the letter-box on the heels of the Christmas cards and anyone not receiving one should send a self-addressed, stamped envelope to a reputable seedsman asking for one to be sent to him.

My advice on making a seed list is to go first for the well-tried varieties that have proved themselves and served you well (including some of the superb veterans) and then to pepper the chosen with some of the exciting novelties. But don't allow yourself to be carried away by the eulogies of the seedsmen.

Every gardener intent on keeping his estate gay from June until October inevitably needs some annuals and half-hardies and perhaps a special border where the flower arranger can cut ruthlessly and fancy-free.

Shrubs

The beginner is inclined to grow anxious if the trees and shrubs he ordered last year have not arrived. Not to worry – there are at least eight good planting weeks ahead.

Greenhouse

Now that the forced spring bulbs are over or indoors the greenhouse will be clearer and can be cleaned and tidied up.

Bedding double lobelia, single is best raised from seed, may be increased by cuttings rooted in light soil.

The hippeastrum (often known as the amaryllis) is encouraged into growth by warmth and watering. This bulbous plant must surely be the most showy, dramatic and fastest grower we have, with its tremendous lily-like flowers in crimson, scarlet and shades of pink.

The bulb can be brought into flower within a month of planting and is all but fool-proof.

It must be kept warm and regularly watered until it has finished growing its strap-like foliage, but when October comes it should be kept cool and dry and put to rest.

Re-potting is only necessary every three years, but the bulb should be top-dressed annually, scraping the tired soil away and replacing it with a rich fresh loam, leaf-mould and sand compost mixture.

Lilies: the ideal time to plant lilies is in the autumn when the soil is still warm from the summer sun. Unfortunately, bulbs are seldom available from the Far East until mid-winter and I haven't the heart to plant them out in the cold. So I suggest placing them in a tray of peat to plump up, later potting them firmly in well-crocked pots half filled with top soil, leaf-mould and sand (the lily has no liking for manure), afterwards placing the pots in the cool greenhouse. It is a joy to bring the lilies into the house when they come into flower.

Whenever possible lily bulbs should be bought from a specialist.

Chrysanthemums: take cuttings of Late Chrysanthemums. Give stools in frames plenty of air and remove discoloured leaves. Cuttings of Decoratives and Singles can be taken now and until mid-February: cuttings from Exhibition varieties should be taken before the end of the month.

Stock plants of chrysanthemums should be sprayed or fumigated with a nicotine insecticide, or a malathion aerosol spray can be used, to control greenfly and leaf miner.

Have you lagged the pipes with felt? If not in use and very severe weather is imminent in the north and cold districts, water should be drained off.

Make sure that you have enough loam, leaf-mould, peat and silver sand for seed sowing, and that the seed boxes are clean and in good repair.

Vegetables

Ventilation is important both for cold frame and greenhouse lettuce and all young green stuff, and prepares the tender for planting out in March.

Sow broad beans and peas in pots for early planting out, sowing outside only in warm districts.

Fruit

Strawberries can now be lightly forced on a top shelf in the greenhouse where they catch the sun.

The bright red stems on the cornus or dog-wood, are seen against the winter flowering heaths.

January
Week 4

Garden flowers

I have just been watching some birds picking out the centre of a polyanthus. Black cotton strung a few inches above the plants will keep them off.

Firm up the newly planted, particularly the roses, after frosts.

As the chrysanthemums become rooted, treat them to individual pots.

A bag of agricultural salt from an agricultural merchant is a wise investment at this time of the year against slippery steps and paths; it also helps to keep the weeds down.

Indoor plants

Hanging baskets are coming back into fashion and with them the achimenes, that was known to the Victorian cottager as the Hot-water Plant. Coming in all tones of red and pinks, blues and violets, it thoroughly deserves this come-back.

The rhizomes may be started any time from January to April and should be planted ¾ in. deep in a free-draining, spongy compost, and do best in a temperature of 15°C. (59°F.).

Having been treated to larger pots when needed, the plant may be finally introduced to the hanging basket, where it mixes happily with the ivy-leaf geraniums and petunias. Alternatively, several rhizomes can be grown in a 5 in. pot, so avoiding any potting on. Always keep in a warm, light place and water with tepid water.

Shrubs

Gardeners looking for tub plants to place either side of the front door should consider the upright and sweet-scented rosemary, that can be gently pinched between finger and thumb as the passer-by goes in and out of the house.

Keep young trees free of grass and weeds at their bases; they will enjoy a dressing of rotted organic matter.

Climbers

Prune and train hardy climbers (including roses) on walls and pergolas.

Greenhouse

Allow for a slight increase in ventilation during the middle of the day, closing down early to retain the warmth.

Gloxinias and begonias in trays should be potted up once they have started in growth.

Strawberries, for an early dish, will appreciate a pinch of nitro-potash.

Chrysanthemums: cuttings of Large Exhibition and Exhibition Incurved taken in early January should now be rooted and ready for potting into 3 in. pots of John Innes Potting Compost No. 2.

Watch the geranium cuttings, discarding those showing any sign of black rot.

Vegetables

Sow tomatoes under glass, carefully spacing the seeds.

Protect sprouts in pigeon-infested areas with netting: these birds have now extended their activities to pecking sprouting broccoli and other green stuff.

Complete the preparation of vegetable plots for sowing.

Gardeners in possession of cloches should stand them over prepared drills to help warm the soil ready for February and early spring sowing.

Potatoes set up in trays for chitting in a frost-proof greenhouse or room for sprouting, should not be allowed more than two sprouts a tuber.

Lettuce can be sown in trays under glass for planting in frames later on.

Fruit

Knobbly stubs on apple trees are often the result of faulty pruning or attacks of woolly aphis. The stubs should be gradually diminished during two or three years, cutting the knobs back to the parent branch and painting the wound with arbrex wound dressing.

Yes, some trees suffer more from incorrect pruning than those left to go their own way.

Give apples and pears a last tar oil winter wash spray, allowing the fluid to drip off the end of the branch.

A weak spray of winter wash against mite on gooseberries will also help to keep the birds away.

Wall subjects, in very cold areas, should be protected from frost; a double layer of old fish netting draped over the plants or sprays of evergreens will serve the purpose.

Cut down newly planted summer-fruiting raspberries to within 6 ins. of the ground and all canes of autumn-fruiting varieties.

Eranthis tubergeniana, the winter buttercup with a green toby collar, and a great deal of charm. Accustomed to growing under trees.

February

The aconite, the winter flowering 'buttercup', with an enchanting green collar, heralds the snowdrops, early this month.

The 14th of February is said to be the galanthus' or snowdrop's birthday. There are sixteen or more species and varieties, both single and double, and being of modest loveliness are best planted in drifts or large groups.

We used to plant snowdrops along with the daffodils when dormant: but now know that they are better moved directly after flowering and before the foliage dies back.

Warning: In spite of the aconites trying to persuade you that winter is over, February is often one of the hardest months of the year.

Digging is the order of the day provided the ground is not wet or frozen. There are often mild spells, quite out of season, when much spring planting can be done.

Pruning should go forward: there is some argument as to whether newly planted trees and shrubs should be pruned before planting or left until March. I prefer to prune before planting, leaving only the pruning of the newly planted rose bushes until later.

May I suggest that when you dive out into the garden for five or ten minutes to have a quick look round, you make a point of carrying out some small job – pulling up a weed or two, examining the efficiency of a tie or the straightness of a stake, firming up a support or a plant loosened by frost, or, on spotting a broken branch, painting the wound with a sealing paint. You'll find something waiting to be done if you keep your eyes open.

Nurserymen suggest that planting can go on until the end of March, but I am not in favour of joining the slowcoaches. Perhaps I should point out that gooseberries should be pruned last at the very end of the month, otherwise the birds will play havoc with both top and lower buds (the lower buds are the last reserve!).

Now to leaf curl – a disease that affects peaches, nectarines, flowering almonds and other prunus. The disease attacks the young leaves, having over-wintered in the buds. Red and pale green patches develop on the foliage, and the leaves thicken, curl and swell. A powdery coating appears on the distorted foliage, which soon turns brown and falls. The loss of the foliage and the energy required to replace it weakens the tree. The infected leaves should be picked off and burnt before the powdery bloom arrives.

It is often too late to do anything helpful when the attack takes place, other than to remove the diseased leaves and burn them.

The control is to spray the tree with a copper fungicide or Bordeaux mixture in early February and again two weeks later just before the buds open. In very cold districts spraying may be delayed for a few weeks.

The affected tree must be sprayed again in the autumn just before leaf fall.

Meanwhile the best place on a nasty February day is the greenhouse, where pests, greenfly and leaf-miner need attention. (Seek out the horrors underneath the leaves.) Cut branches of forsythia and flowering currant (if you don't dislike their pungent scent) and plunge them deep in a bucket for early flowering in the house.

The decks can be cleared of faded spring flowers, and the peaches disbudded and pollinated by the gardener aping the function of the busy bee with a camel-hair brush.

The chrysanthemum fan, always at the ready with a knife in his pocket, will not find himself at a loss, and can take yet another cutting.

16

Snowdrops at Kew.

February
Week 1

Garden flowers

Firm up the wallflowers lifted by the frost, and replace any casualties with plants from the nursery bed if the weather is kind.

There is still time to divide the large clumps of Michaelmas daisies and perennials in the border, keeping the vigorous outside growth and discarding the tired centre. Some plants allow themselves to be torn apart, others are better divided by using two forks back to back. The paeony and scabious must be left undisturbed: they may sulk with resentment when deranged.

Keep the slug bait handy and protect tulips and tempting fresh green growth. It is the stationary and slow moving beasties that are the garden enemies, such as the slug and wireworm: the fast moving, the ladybird and others, are our helpful friends.

Shrubs

Summer-flowering shrubs can be kept shapely by cutting them back to an outward bud close to the base of last year's growth. Left to themselves they make larger shrubs, but the stems and flower spikes suffer in vigour. The buddleias or butterfly bushes, in particular, respond to severe pruning.

Greenhouse

Seed sowing starts in earnest this month.

Pans, boxes (not more than 3 ins. in depth), staging and the water tank should all be ready and hospital clean.

Seed boxes or containers should be well drained and filled with John Innes Potting Compost No. 1 or crumbly loam (the top $\frac{1}{4}$ in. must be finely sieved).

The seed should be sown as thinly as possible to avoid damping off. Very small seed, such as the gloxinia, should be placed on the surface of the soil and only lightly covered with sand: the larger seeds, such as the nasturtium and lupin, are better planted $\frac{1}{4}$ in. deep and sprinkled with sand. Finally press the seed down firmly with a flat board, water with a fine rose-can, and leave the container to drain. Cover the pan or box with glass and paper. All seeds germinate best in darkness.

The soil must be kept slightly moist until the seedlings appear.

Half-hardy annuals are normally raised from sowings made in a warm greenhouse from early February until the end of April. They call for more attention than the hardy, and success depends much on hardening them off (acclimatizing them to outdoor conditions) without checking their growth.

The half-hardy annuals complete their life-cycle within the space of a season. If the gardener has neither greenhouse nor frame, he can sow outdoors in late March (waiting until April in the north and cold parts of the country).

Make a point of taking a final batch of decorative and single chrysanthemum cuttings.

Vegetables

Rhubarb can be planted or divided this month using a rich prepared soil.

Prepare for onions: a fine tilth is all-important for the gardener wishing to exhibit.

Plant Jerusalem artichokes and shallots, burying their tails just below soil level in hiding from the birds.

Some annual weeds may rear their unwanted heads, and hoeing may be necessary between crops not yet ready to clear.

Where mice are a menace, a few mousetraps suitably baited should be placed in an open-ended tin or drainpipe out of sight of the birds.

Fruit

Keep the bullfinches and other birds away from the gooseberry buds as best you can. A fruit cage pays dividends.

All autumn-fruiting raspberry canes should be cut down to within 5 ins. of the ground to encourage young growth to bear fruit next season.

Complete fruit tree planting as soon as possible.

Tar oil spraying must stop before buds open.

Crocus tomasinianus, the silvery lilac species, known to its friends as Tommy, that will willingly naturalize and seed itself in the grass.

February
Week 2

Garden flowers

Sow sweet peas in their flowering positions. If you have not time to grow them as cordons, sow the seed in bush formation. The flowers won't be as large, but they will smell as sweet.

Bring in the last of the spring bulbs from the plunge bed.

Members of the herbaceous border, such as the hardy chrysanthemums, will appreciate attention; they are hardy, but vulnerable to waterlogging after a storm or heavy rainfall.

Shrubs

Complete all work and transplanting in the shrubbery so that you can give your full attention to the sowing and planting programme just coming up.

Climbers

Pruning clematis is confusing for beginners, but to simplify the undertaking, varieties that flower on the current year's growth, such as the lovely summer-flowering purple Jackmanii, the viticella types and the late-flowering species should be cut back to within 12 ins. of the base in February or early March.

The May and June large-flowered hybrids, including the popular Nellie Moser and the double and semi-double varieties, that flower on the previous year's wood, should be kept in place, but only lightly pruned. Weak wood may be thinned out and the growths left shortened to a strong pair of buds.

Greenhouse

Keep watering to a minimum until you are sure spring has arrived.

It is a mistake to sow all your half-hardies early: sow the slow-growing lobelias, begonias, pansies and others first, and leave the petunias, nemesias, and fast-growing marigolds until mid-March: otherwise they are apt to get leggy and outstay their time in the greenhouse.

Begonia tubers can be started in growth any time from January to early May, but if glass and heat are not available, it is advisable to wait until mid-March. A temperature of 16° to 18°C. (61°–64°F.) is necessary.

The tubers must be covered, but not be completely buried, in moist compost or peat so that roots are encouraged all over the surface of the tuber.

When the growths have reached about 2½ ins. they should be reduced to two shoots a plant. Once well rooted the plants should be treated to individual 6 in. pots.

Young fibrous-rooted begonias from cuttings should not be allowed to flower at an early stage: buds should be pinched out until the plant has built up a sturdy constitution.

Over-wintered fuchsias and geraniums should be re-potted or potted on, and heliotrope encouraged into growth by warmth and occasional spraying.

Chrysanthemum stools should now be providing cuttings. These should be taken below a leaf joint, dipped in a rooting powder, and kept close in gentle warmth. (A polythene bag is helpful if the propagating box is full.) Make a point of taking a final batch of decoratives and singles.

Seed boxes should be inspected regularly and both glass and paper removed once germination has taken place.

Vegetables

The plot to be used for green crops may need liming: a test kit will give the answer. Spent crops should be cleared and the lime applied to the soil surface: it should be lightly hoed in or the wind will blow it away.

Ground intended for roots should be dressed once with 4 ozs. of a mixture of 3 lbs. of superphosphate, 1½ lbs. of sulphate of potash and ¾ lb. of sulphate of ammonia per sq. yd. This should be hoed in a week or so before sowing.

Tomatoes for growing outdoors can be sown in the greenhouse if a temperature of 16°–18°C. (61°–64°F.) can be maintained (otherwise, it is a waste of time).

Fruit

If a tree is suffering badly from disease, it is better grubbed up and burnt. It is a mistake to turn your garden into a nursing home.

Canker can be spread from one tree to another. If a limb is severely affected, it should be ruthlessly removed (and the wound dressed) rather than disfigured by a series of incisions.

General

If you burn everything that can't be put on the compost heap, you will be surprised to find how straight and tidy the garden looks. Meanwhile keep the bonfire ash dry and give it to your favourite vegetable or fruit tree.

Skimmia japonica berries defeat the snow. A slow-growing compact plant that enjoys a place in the shade.

February
Week 3

Garden flowers

Any dahlia tubers showing a mildew should be rubbed with a dry rag and re-dusted with sulphur (decay should be cut out).

Hardy annuals sown under cloches will give a fine display towards the end of the summer. Don't forget the larkspurs, if you want flowers for cutting.

Sweet peas can be sown under cloches in the north and in the open ground in the south. Seed should be sown 2 ins. deep.

Go on picking the Algerian iris for the nosegay on your desk, but do not in spontaneous appreciation feed or cosset the plant for it revels in poor soil and starvation.

Shrubs

If necessary to keep them shapely and to size, take the shears to the winter heathers as soon as the flowers have faded. Any summer-flowering ones, that have not been trimmed, should have their annual light clipping now.

Don't be afraid to do some last minute planting (up to the middle of March), but choose a mild day and make sure the roots are kept moist until safely in the ground.

Climbers

The summer-flowering jasmine, *Jasminum officinale*, should be thinned out.

Hedges

Deciduous hedges may be planted in well-prepared ground during a mild spell.

Weeds that grow so luxuriously beneath the hedge are easily killed with simazine put down in winter or by watering them with paraquat in spring and summer.

Overgrown hedges can be cut hard back at the end of the month.

Greenhouse

The gloxinia can be started into growth from January until March: if without glass and heat, it is wiser to wait until the later date.

Place the tubers just below the surface of the soil, using a compost of equal parts of fibrous peat, loam, leaf-mould and well-decayed manure, with a sprinkling of silver sand. Keep the plant close to the glass, watering moderately until growth is well advanced, afterwards freely applying weak liquid manure when buds arrive.

The fuchsia wakes up in February and should be pruned, moved into a warmer temperature and given a light position where it will get the morning sun. The plant should be sprayed with tepid water night and morning, and treated to mild doses of liquid manure once flower buds have formed.

Bud dropping, about which I get so many complaints, is due to fluctuating temperature – hot days followed by cold nights.

Check the stored gladioli corms and dust with BHC if disease is suspected. The corms can be sprouted in moderate heat, 10°–12°C. (50°–54°F.) in pots or boxes.

When the freesias are over the pots should be laid on their sides to dry off.

Some of the early summer-flowering seedlings will now be ready for pricking out.

Vegetables

Stump carrots can be sown in frames.

Successional sowings of tomatoes should be made.

Turnips and spinach can be sown outdoors, but at your own risk.

Parsnips can be sown and benefit by a long-growing season.

Herbs

Parsley should be sown in a sheltered place.

Fruit

Vine spurs in the greenhouse should be limited to one last season's shoot. The buds will enjoy a light syringing with tepid water at noon on a sunny day, but they must be dry by evening time. Do not encourage young growth by high temperatures: young shoots are undesirable while there is still danger of frost.

Prune cobnuts and filberts once you have spotted the small red female flowers that often go unnoticed among the eye-catching male catkins.

Lawn

Fallen leaves and wormcasts should be brushed away with a besom throughout January and February and the turf not walked upon when frozen or wet.

If wormcasts are trodden in, they will clog and damage the turf.

A moderate worm population in the garden is desirable, but the lawn is better without them, so if there are too many, a killer with a mowrah base will eradicate them. Sweeping up the corpses is an extremely unpleasant chore and many gardeners prefer to dodge it by using chlordane that kills the worms below ground. It must be remembered that this product is poisonous.

Crocus chrysanthus 'Cream Beauty', with striking orange-scarlet stigmata, one of the gems of the family.

February
Week 4

Shrubs

Buds are swelling and the time for planting trees, shrubs and roses will soon be coming to an end.

Gardeners in the south and warmer gardens can begin to prune their roses leisurely.

Examine all stakes and ties against March winds.

Greenhouse

Dahlias that have been stored through the winter can now be started into growth in a cool house: covered with leaf-mould and peat and kept moist, they will soon provide young growth for cuttings or division.

The shoot can be taken when 3 to 4 ins. either with the 'eye' or severed below a node when the eye will provide further cuttings. A rooting powder is helpful, and a mixture of peat and silver sand serves as a good rooting medium.

When the cutting perks up and has established roots it may be treated to a 3 or 3½ in. pot, using John Innes Potting Compost No. 1.

Although a temperature of 7°–12°C. (45°–54°F.) satisfies many plants, for the germination of seeds and rooting of cuttings over 12°C. (54°F.) is desirable.

Use a propagating frame, maybe a do-it-yourself affair (a humble polythene bag or sheet will fill the bill), but of course the electric soil heating cable that gives bottom heat is the ideal.

Make sure there is a small supply of John Innes Potting Compost No. 2 for the second potting of rooted chrysanthemum cuttings.

Keep the chrysanthemums frost-proof, but cool.

Large Exhibition and Incurved should be repotted in 5 in. pots when their roots require more room, using John Innes Potting Compost No. 2. They should be transferred to a protected frame as soon as they have recovered from the move.

Potted hydrangeas may be sprayed, given more warmth, and started into growth.

Young cyclamen should be kept growing: old corms will take a rest after flowering and should be gradually dried off and placed on their sides.

Cuttings can be taken from Busy Lizzie and winter-flowering begonias.

This is the right time for re-potting or top-dressing the majority of house plants. Ordinary garden soil is seldom rich enough to sustain the confined pot plant. It can be replaced or improved by adding: 1 part leaf-mould or peat, 1 part sharp sand, plus 3 ozs. of John Innes base fertilizer per bushel. Meanwhile John Innes Potting Compost No. 1, plus an addition of granulated peat (1 part to every 2–3 of compost, depending upon the plant in question) suits most house plants.

Vegetables

Sow cauliflower, quick-maturing cabbage, summer spinach and lettuce under glass.

Autumn onions can be transplanted and set 18 ins. apart.

Prick out the onion seedlings, treating some of them to small individual pots, if you are interested in size and exhibiting. Shade should be given from bright sun until the seedlings are established.

When preparing for peas find a well-drained, deeply dug plot that has been manured for the previous crop and with a lime content.

Make first sowing of peas in cold districts and sow in succession outdoors from now until June.

A sheltered spot should be found for a sowing of rounded peas.

Don't hurry to put out the seed potatoes if the weather is cold. Shoots on stored potatoes should be rubbed off.

Cloches are urgently needed this month for beetroot, brussels, lettuce, carrots, peas (rather a risky sowing) and potatoes.

The gardener should get in the habit of successional sowing; in other words, little and often, making the packets go a long way.

Beware of slugs in mild spells, particularly under cloches. Slug pellets should be placed along the rows.

Herbs

With so much tasteless food on our plates, from tin or freezer, we appreciate the flavour and virtues of herbs. Herb plantings are springing up in tubs, window-boxes, roof gardens, in between the spokes of old cartwheels and other specially designed beds.

Mint, rue, parsley, chives, sage, tarragon, fennel, thyme and rosemary can all be planted now.

I have a passion for parsley. It is easily raised from seed. The veteran gardener still waters the drill with boiling water before sowing, but the Wisley-trained gardener smiles at the thought.

Most herbs are easily bought from seedsmen: but the specialist wishing for the rarer plants, such as lovage and the aromatic costmary, must seek a herb nursery.

Herbs love the sun: in Old Adam's language they should be planted within spitting distance of the kitchen.

Plant garlic.

Lift a root of mint and fit it in at the end of a line of cloches.

Fruit

Pruning of plums and spraying with winter wash must be completed.

Sow melons in heat.

Salix medemii, a shrubby willow, with fascinating yellow catkins in February and March.

March

Weather varies more in March than in any other month of the year. Gardeners in the north must take the time-lag due to the colder temperatures into account before sowing. In areas where the temperature falls below 6°C. (43°F.), plants, and even the turf, will wait to grow until April.

Meanwhile, the low rainfall and the drying winds result in good gardening weather, and there is no longer an excuse for delaying the digging. Make a point of skimming off the weeds first, burying them below ground as you go.

Borders can be tidied up, stems cut down and the soil dressed with hoof and horn meal.

If there are gaps to fill, the budget will dictate the choice: a 10p. packet of seed, marigold, candytuft or nasturtium, will meet the need, but if a tree paeony can be afforded, then glamour will be added to the border.

May I remind the novice when spring-cleaning the herbaceous border that the paeony, scabious, and the *Alstromeria ligtu* hybrids should be left strictly alone: they resent disturbance and demonstrate their feelings by sulking. Bearded iris are happier when moved and divided after flowering.

Rampant growers should be treated severely, in particular the aggressive Michaelmas daisy, rudbeckia, solidago, and saponaria.

Mowing machines and other tools sent for overhaul should now be brought back from the ironmongers. I have noticed the veteran gardener trying out his mower before leaving the shop by placing a sheet of paper through the machine to make sure the cut and set is sharp and clean.

Much time will be spent this month in seed sowing and hardening off seedlings.

The gardener should now give his attention to interesting and attractive flower associations: the painter's palette is in his hand, and it is for him to see that every group and drift of flowers enhance each other.

Many of our annuals deserve exciting companions, among them the splendid little lobelia condemned for generations to be the inevitable bedfellow of scarlet geraniums and white alyssum. This brilliant small flower should be planted in blocks and drifts rather than in institutional lines, and will play an important part in a blue border along with phacelia, nemophilia, love-in-a-mist, with delphiniums and the novelty blue and 'aluminium' eryngium in the background.

Not everybody has the space for a blue border, but there is always room for a blue patch. I once filled my London window-box with blocked Oxford and Cambridge lobelia in a pleasing pattern: it was long-lasting, trouble free and a smash hit.

Plantings depend on taste: there will be those who go for pale shades, and a pale planting with a backing of becoming green foliage is delightful. But there are others who will prefer the garish and would enjoy a border, such as I saw in Scotland long ago, of red and orange – and so garish that the thought of it still makes me blink.

I cannot over-stress the importance of fine tilth for successful sowing. The seed that lands on a clod has an under-privileged youth.

Seedlings must be pricked out before they jostle each other, otherwise they will grow tall and spindly, and never fully recover.

Hardening off should begin at an early stage, accustoming seedlings to the cooler outdoor conditions before planting out.

Frame lights may be lifted a little higher every day until they can be removed altogether. If the seedlings turn colour or stop growing, beware!

Spring flowers.

March
Week 1

Garden flowers

Seed sowing can begin if the weather is friendly: a general fertilizer, 2 ozs. to the sq. yd., should be worked into the bed for annuals and half-hardies.

Gardeners in the south, who have hardened off their sweet pea seedlings, can now plant them out during a mild spell. Those in the north must be more patient. The drills should be watered the day previously and the roots carefully disentangled before planting.

Care should be taken that the brown mark or collar above the seed stem is left visible and not buried. Finally, a few bushy twigs should be placed around each plant.

Sweet pea seed can now be sown 1–1½ ins. deep outdoors. Beware of mice!

Many herbaceous plants should be restricted at an early stage to 6–8 shoots a plant.

Shrubs

When should roses be pruned? This is the most controversial subject among rosarians, but the majority agree that mid-February in the south to mid-April in the north is the best time – when the sap begins to rise. But there are many who prune in December or January and are confident that this leads to earlier and larger blooms. Much will depend on climate and weather.

The aim of the operation should be to keep the bush open to light and air, dismissing dead or crossing branches and weak wood.

Moderate pruning is advised, tackling the strongest varieties first. The floribunda is probably the most difficult bush to prune satisfactorily; light pruning of young wood and moderate pruning of older wood should result in the bush flowering continuously throughout the summer.

There are no absolute rules and the weak plant is often a problem child: in this event commonsense must play its part.

Many shrubs can be pruned now to within 1–2 ins. of last year's growth; the resulting growth will bear next year's flowers.

Reminder: buddleia and *hydrangea paniculata* should be cut back hard to within a few inches of the ground, or in the case of old plants, to the previous season's wood.

Greenhouse

Half-hardies – asters, French marigolds, stocks, petunias and others – should be sown in a warm greenhouse or the kitchen. They should be pricked out when the first true leaves open.

Geraniums should be repotted, or potted on, using a fibrous loam, half part well-decayed manure, half part leaf-mould and one part coarse sand, adding a tablespoonful of superphosphate, or a ¼ part of bonemeal to each bushel (equal to a good pailful). Boxed-up plants should be potted up separately. The plants should be watered moderately for the first ten days after re-potting and a watch kept for white fly.

Vegetables

Choose the first mild day for large scale sowing when the soil can be easily worked. Onions come first!

The preparation and fine tilth of the onion bed is all-important. I always remember the old gardener, who moved house, carting and taking his onion bed with him.

The main sowing of celery should be made.

Tomato seedlings should be potted into 3 in. pots as soon as they are large enough to handle.

Fruit

A dressing of Growmore, 2–4 ozs. per sq. yard, followed by a mulch of compost, will be welcomed by all bush fruit. Gooseberries and red and black currants appreciate an additional dressing of sulphate of potash, 1–2 ozs. to the sq. yard.

Prune newly planted black currants; gooseberries and red currants are lightly pruned to enable the plant to build up a good bush framework. Established bushes are often left unpruned until later for fear of bird pecking.

More strawberries can be planted, but they must not be allowed to flower in their first year.

Camellia 'Furo-an', a single-flowered beauty hardy in sheltered gardens, but should be given protection until established.

March
Week 2

Garden flowers

Plant out wallflowers and forget-me-nots, and fill any gaps in formal plantings from the nursery beds.

Snowdrops can be divided; we have learned that they are better lifted when green and growing than when dormant.

More sweet peas can be sown now. Heavy or unappetising soil can be improved by applying burnt earth, grit, leaf-mould, peat or anything of an opening or friable nature. Seed should be sown 1–1½ ins. deep.

Shrubs

Roots of trees, including fruit and shrubs, arriving from the nursery when weather conditions do not permit planting, are quick to dry out; they must be soaked in a bucket of water before planting.

Greenhouse

Young fuchsias should be potted on when needing more root room. Old plants should have the soil removed from the roots and may well benefit by being given a smaller pot.

Youngsters that arrive in 3 in. pots are best left in their containers for a few days so that they can be freely watered and rested. Fuchsias are not fussy about soil provided the loam is good and there is liquid feeding regularly, starting two weeks after potting. Boots' Compure K., used according to instructions given, is a fine tonic.

John Innes Base fertilizer, peat and silver sand with a sprinkling of powdered chalk, is used as a potting compost by many successful growers.

Trimming and shaping may start in February (taking the growing points out of shoots); pinching should continue until 6 or 7 weeks before the plant is required to flower.

Many fuchsias fall by the wayside through irregular watering when planted out. The occasional shower does not replace the daily watering can.

Cuttings can be taken as they present themselves at any time of the year, but strike best in autumn or spring when the sun is not too hot.

Rooted cuttings of early flowering chrysanthemums should be transplanted either in trays (at least 3 ins. deep), or in beds in the frames. Decoratives should be potted on into 4½ in. pots as soon as their present ones are full of roots and moved to the frame.

Primula obconica may be sown in a temperature of 15°–17°C. (59°–63°F.). The new apple blossom varieties are particularly beautiful.

Vegetables

Seed sowing should now be in full swing. After the onions, come broad beans, parsnips, lettuce, radish, early carrots, shallots and onion sets. Summer spinach should be found a warm corner.

Prick over the seed bed for the last time, working in a little peat or compost, adding a sprinkling of general fertilizer if the ground is poor.

Brussels sprouts can be sown in a warm greenhouse.

Broad beans may be sown in boxes for planting out later on.

Cucumbers usually do best sown this month.

Rhubarb and horseradish can be planted now, but the latter must be controlled, otherwise it is difficult to get rid of when once established.

Fruit

March weather seldom encourages insects and the gardener, with camel-hair brush or rabbit's tail in hand, must do his best to imitate the bee in pollinating the peaches, moving the pollen from flower to flower.

Tar oil spraying in the orchard should now be complete. Slow-coaches and those who have not had the opportunity to carry out the work before, can stretch a point and spray this week, but only if buds are still dormant.

Pieris forrestii, one of my favourite shrubs: the young growth is brilliant red: the large panicles of bronze buds open to ivory flowers.

March
Week 3

Garden flowers

Lupin and delphinium shoots can be taken from the crown, dipped in rooting powder and inserted in pots of sandy compost and placed in the greenhouse. They should be kept close, but do not require heat.

Gladioli should be planted at intervals of a fortnight from the middle of March to April: they take about ninety days from planting to flowering.

Corms should be planted in groups, 6–9 ins. apart, and 4–5 ins. deep; cushions of sharp sand at the base of the corms will help to prevent rotting.

The gardener should stake early and give the plants a good soaking once a week, stirring the top soil so that the water soaks in, after which the plants should be mulched around their roots to prevent moisture from evaporating. Dribs and drabs of water are to be avoided. After flowering, watering should cease.

Gladioli for cutting are best planted in the vegetable garden, for once they have flowered they lose their appearance. Leaves should be left when picking the stem.

Small flowered types, the hooded primulinus and the butterflies provide a wide range of colour in different shades and have more charm than their big brothers.

Shrubs

The beginner should go round his rosebeds a second time to make sure he has left no dead or crossing branches: the best roses cannot be expected from old hard wood. He must also make sure all newly planted bushes are firm in the ground.

Roses should be given a rose fertilizer at the rate the manufacturers recommend.

Preparations should be made for planting evergreens and conifers.

Hedges

Have the shears been sharpened? Privet and lonicera hedges will soon need attention. Laurel should be trimmed with secateurs to avoid mutilation of leaves.

Greenhouse

Chrysanthemums, dahlias and bedding plants will now be moving on from greenhouse to the frame to harden off. A fortunate exit, for the tomatoes will be hankering to take their place, demanding a temperature of 12°–15°C. (54°–59°F.).

Decorative chrysanthemums should be re-potted into $4\frac{1}{2}$ in. pots as soon as the 3 in. pots become full of roots: they can then be transferred to the frame.

Dahlia cuttings of 3–4 ins. may be taken. Taken with a heel a hundred percent 'strike' may be expected, but of course there will be fewer cuttings.

Heliotrope or cherry pie cuttings will root in a sandy soil if kept close.

Repot or top-dress the aspidistra, maidenhair and other ferns.

Fuchsias should be regularly pinched back and the prunings used as cuttings.

Sow herbaceous perennials in frame or greenhouse, covering the seeds with finely sieved soil, shading them from sunlight until germination.

Delphinium seed bought from a specialist is a worthwhile investment.

Some of the annuals make desirable pot plants; among them are the stocks which give a drench of fragrance.

Stake and tie growing plants early rather than late: schizanthus need regular training.

Vegetables

After the onions and parsnips, peas, broad beans, lettuce and radishes should be sown in rich soil at intervals of 10–12 days.

Half-inch drills suit most small seeds, sowing the peas in a flat drill a little deeper than the rest.

French beans may be sown in frames or in open, previously prepared ground and covered with cloches.

Beds should now be ready for sowing brussels, cabbage and cauliflower to be transplanted later on.

Celery can be sown, also leeks (under glass, if possible).

Watch out for carrot fly.

Fruit

Recently planted fruit trees should be kept free of grass and weeds at their base: they need all the nourishment and nitrogen they can get.

In cold districts bloom on wall peaches and others may be damaged by spring frosts. Protection can be given by covering the trees with a double thickness of netting. The covering should be removed every day when the temperature rises above freezing point. Some gardeners protect the blossom with spruce shoots placed among the branches.

New strawberry plants can still be planted, but must not be allowed to fruit this season.

Raspberry canes recently planted should be reduced to 12–18 ins., according to their vigour.

Anemone apennina makes a striking carpet of lavender blue daisy-like flowers. It should be planted in early March.

March
Week 4

Garden flowers

Protect crocus, polyanthus and wisteria from birds with black cotton or spray with bird repellent: unfortunately, re-spraying is necessary after heavy rainfall.

Chrysanthemums: beds prepared for the early flowering should be given a light dressing of John Innes Base fertilizer, 1–1½ ozs. to the sq. yard.

Indoor plants

House plants can be re-started into growth by watering and a little more heat.

Feeding can begin once the plants show new growth, but never feed when the soil is dry or the plant in bad health or resting: most plants rest in the winter from September to April. Over-feeding is a temptation: the manufacturer's instructions should be followed, or you will be in trouble. Give a little less rather than more, and no double doses. The meanest of men becomes madly generous with the fertilizer tin.

Shrubs

Trees and shrubs will appreciate a mulch of light straw-manure: heavy slabs should be broken down. Newcomers benefit when planting, if given a generous amount of peat: there are peat haters, but they are in a minority.

Complete planting of shrubs and roses other than the evergreens or container-grown.

Rose pruning should be completed except in northern and very exposed gardens, where it may continue until mid-April.

Heathers are easily layered in March.

Climbers

Thin out the exotic passion flower, removing weak shoots and shortening strong ones by one-third.

Greenhouse

Ventilation is made difficult by winds: beware of draughts and using other than top ventilators unless the temperature jumps up at a suspicion of the sun.

China asters and any unsuccessful spring sowing of bedding plants should be re-sown.

The schizanthus should be potted on before it becomes root-bound.

January-sown sweet peas should be stopped, pinching out the second pair of leaves immediately they open.

Plants that have been hardened off in a frame can be planted out, protecting them from slugs and birds.

Chrysanthemums: all late flowering singles should be given the first 'stop' by April 14th (10 days after the second potting).

Stopping dates, important to the serious grower, are given in the National Chrysanthemum Society's diary. The diary, available from the Secretary of the Society only, is valuable to the enthusiast.

Vegetables

The first sowing of vegetables should now be completed, and seedlings that have been hardened off can be planted out.

Gardeners in the north can plant out shallots (but potatoes should only be risked in the warmer gardens unless they can be given protection). Earlies only are worth this risk and trouble.

They can be planted through slits, made a foot apart in strips of black polythene, laid on the ground, which keeps down weeds, the soil moist and its temperature higher. The potato plants as they grow push up through them.

Lettuce must be hardened off carefully: all the early sown benefit by spending a final few weeks in the cold frame.

Herbs

Chives can be divided and replanted.

Fruit

Peaches and nectarines should be sprayed with lime sulphur or colloidal copper against leaf curl.

Tidy up the strawberries removing all discoloured leaves, and lightly fork in a sprinkling of fertilizer.

Lawn

Lawn care starts in earnest this month: brushing, raking, and piercing the turf with a fork when weather permits. A roller should be seldom used and never when the lawn is wet: it should not weigh more than 2 cwt. for fear of compacting the soil and turf.

Mowing, with blades high, should be limited to two cuts in March, giving a rake between the two mowings, so that the grass stands up to meet the blades and is only topped.

The new lawn should not be cut until 3 ins. high.

Polyanthus pacific, a robust strain with strong stems and tremendous 'pips' that are the result of controlled breeding over many years.

April

This is the month of hope and anticipation.

Warm sunshine is often followed by frost at night and should you be caught napping and a plant frozen, it should be thawed out by spraying with tepid water, afterwards covering it with bracken or paper.

If on heavy land, there are those, among them the scabious, that are safer planted in spring than autumn.

Successional sowings can be made of annuals in the kitchen garden to avoid picking from beds and borders.

Running water and pools are much in fashion. The gardener should prepare for waterside planting next month. A drift of golden marsh marigolds, forget-me-nots, *Myosotis palustris*, and white and glorious yellow sunrise water lilies, with a few willows in the background with flat-faced Japanese iris at their feet makes a happy picture.

Meanwhile, back to earth, this is the month to make war on weeds.

The gardener should look out for the Easter performer, the Pasque flower, an enchanting mauve flower decked with silky hairs and filigree foliage: if you live on the pulsatilla's favourite chalk soil, you must not fail to grow it.

As many nurseries as possible should be visited and, perhaps, Kew and Wisley when the ornamental cherries are in full bloom. The cherries are a great sight, from rather crude double-pink Kanzan of by-pass renown, to the more distinguished white prunus, *Avium flore plena*, one of the loveliest of them all. These visits will help you in making your list for autumn planting.

Spring bulb planting is the keen gardener's regular autumn chore, but comparatively few plant the summer-flowering bulbs in late March, and by not doing so miss a lot. May I remind you of the Caen anemones, the single poppy flowers with black centres, and the richly coloured St. Brigids, the galtonias or summer hyacinths, the exotic tigridias in exciting colours, and others that deserve to be seen more.

Spring-flowering shrubs that have bloomed, and in particular the free-growing forsythia, can be pruned; and any last planting of rhododendrons or azaleas made towards the end of the month, tucking the roots up in plenty of peat.

Now to the greenhouse where the schizanthus should be soon at the top of its form, with the calceolarias not far behind them.

The temperature must not be allowed to rise above 18°C. (64°F.) otherwise the cinerarias and the sensitive plants will wilt (damping down the floors and in between the pots may be the answer). Meanwhile, ventilate the house in the morning, closing up at about 4 p.m.

April is a busy time, for nearly all greenhouse plants can be propagated this month, and the pot-bound will be crying out for attention.

Be ready to shade against sunshine and fumigate or spray with nicotine immediately pests are spotted.

This is also one of the busiest months in the vegetable garden. Don't make the mistake of leaving everything until the Easter holidays.

The time for sowing in the open ground will depend on the weather: far better wait until the earth has dried out than sow when it is cold and wet.

Where apple or pear scab is rampant, an anti-scab spray should be given during the early part of the month.

A lime sulphur spray at pink bud stage should be followed by a nicotine spray if pests are still active.

In fairness to the bee avoid spraying when the flowers are open.

Meanwhile, if time permits, a visit to the Azalea Bowl in Windsor Park will be of particular interest to gardeners on acid soil.

A cottage garden in spring.

April
Week 1

Garden flowers

Whenever possible choose a showery day for planting out seedlings: twigs give support to the weak.

I am in favour of lifting a few dark-coloured polyanthus, potting them up for early flowering in the greenhouse. The dark colours respond better than the pastel shades that often lack colour when grown under glass. Forget-me-nots can also be lifted and potted up in the greenhouse: they make good temporary house plants while in flower.

All spring bulbs that have flowered can be transferred to the frame for a week or so: it seems rather brutal to turn them straight out of the house and the greenhouse into the cold garden.

It is hoped that the herbaceous border has been weeded and the large clumps divided. Don't be in a hurry to plant out the dahlias.

The pampas grass when quite dry can be dismissed by burning.

Iris unguicularis can be planted now: September is the easiest time to divide when transplanting in the border.

Plant a last batch of butterfly gladioli, for cutting.

Weed and replant when necessary in the rock garden. Garden centres will now be offering small plants in containers. The crocks from the root ball should be removed and the plants dropped in without much disturbance. A collection of aubrietas is preferable to a planting of the over-familiar mauve variety, and a series of mossy and encrusted saxifrages, houseleeks, or campanulas add interest.

Shrubs

Spring drought can be a killer to the newly planted and the spring winds more drying than those of summer. The newcomers should be re-mulched after a downpour and not allowed to dry out until they are established and able to look after themselves.

Greenhouse

Basal cuttings of about 2 ins. can be taken from the summer-flowering begonias.

Don't allow the Indian azalea to go dry: if threatening to burst its container it should be repotted, using a peat and fibrous loam compost with a sprinkling of coarse sand. Being a lime hater, the azalea prefers soft rainwater to a drink from the tap.

Chrysanthemums: Large Exhibition, Paul Hapgood and Mark Woolman, should be stopped about April 14th. The list of stoppings should now be regularly consulted.

House plants are best kept close in the greenhouse after re-potting. Should the foliage flop, shade for a few days and syringe with tepid water.

Freesias should be dried off, gradually cutting down the water supply. Cyclamen and lachenalias should be given the same treatment.

Vegetables

Potatoes: apply complete fertilizer mixture of 3 lbs. of superphosphate, 1½ lb. of sulphate of potash and 1½ lb. of sulphate of ammonia at 2–3 ozs. to the yard run of the drills at planting time. Complete the planting of the earlies.

Whenever frost threatens, potato tips should be lightly covered with soil. Should they go on growing, protect the young growth with straw.

Spring cabbage will benefit by an application of nitro chalk (2 ozs. per yard run). Apply in showery weather, keeping the foliage clear for fear of burning.

Brussels sprouts should be planted out on a rich loam that has been well fed for a previous crop. The soil should be trodden firm (loose soil results in blown sprouts). Failing rain, watering may be necessary.

Another sowing of French beans can be made for a continuity crop.

Fruit

Spraying blackcurrants with lime sulphur against big bud should not be delayed. It is not necessary to wait, as we are often told, until the leaves reach the size of a shilling. Beware of sulphur-shy varieties and use a weaker solution.

Lawn

From now on, the lawn will require regular attention, aerating and mowing right through the summer.

Prunus domestica, the common almond, early to bloom and the best flowering tree for towns.

April
Week 2

Garden flowers

Annuals will germinate well now.

I have no sense of heresy in sowing a few annuals in the rock garden and can recommend a patch of bright blue *Phacelia campanulata* to enliven the scene when the spring alpines are over.

A dressing of weathered soot, applied to a damp soil at 3 ozs. to a sq. yd., will darken and help to warm it up. The soot must be stored and mellowed under cover for three months before it can be used with safety.

Plant any gladioli left over for successional cutting.

Prepare window-boxes, tubs and other garden containers with a rich compost for planting.

Fork a sprinkling of bonemeal into the soil around the rock plants.

Shrubs

When evergreen planting is completed, try your hand at layering. Rhododendron, Pink Pearl, or any other free-growing commoner, lends itself well for this task. Choose a pliable branch of last year's growth that will willingly bend to soil level: after making a slit on the underside of the branch, press the incision down into a small heap of peaty-loam that has been generously sprinkled with sand, and hold firm with a stake.

I was taught the art of layering before I could read adequately, my father being a rhododendron enthusiast: at the time I found it a very dull game. However, I have grown to find it both fascinating and rewarding.

The layer should be kept slightly moist until it makes growth – a sign that it has taken root. Don't be impatient to separate the youngster from its parent.

Go round the roses, for the last time, with pruning knife in hand: it is possible you did not deal severely enough with the shy varieties, and leaving weak growth on the bush is a mistake.

Having completed pruning, the bushes should be given a feed. The well-known Tonk's Rose Fertilizer is hard to beat when applied at 3 ozs. a sq. yd. You can buy it ready-mixed, but if you wish to make your own, here is the formula:

10 parts nitrate of potash
12 parts superphosphate of lime
 8 parts sulphate of ammonia
 1 part sulphate of iron
 2 parts sulphate of magnesium

Greenhouse

Beware of opening side ventilators: half-hardy seedlings are particularly vulnerable to draught.

Pests now rear their ugly heads: there is no one cure-all application, and advice should be sought. Liquid contact and systemic controls are helpful, while derris and pyrethrum have the advantage of being non-poisonous aids.

Young cyclamen should be potted on when necessary without checking their growth.

Zinnias are tricky customers and several sowings in frame and greenhouse should be made to avoid disappointment.

Offsets from many of the house plants can be detached: if they have a heel or rootlet, so much the better.

A basket of pendular fuchsias will be found rewarding.

Chrysanthemums: early-flowering varieties that need early stopping will require attention by April 20th. Spraying should be stopped to encourage flowering.

Vegetables

Thin any vegetable seedlings that are in danger of growing leggy through overcrowding.

Prepare for further sowings and trenches for celery.

Catch-crops of radishes and lettuce can be sown between pea rows and in odd corners.

Asparagus can be planted now: speedy planting on a dull day is advised, covering the plants with soil so they do not dry out. If on heavy soil, the bed should be raised.

Onions for pickling may be allocated to the less cultivated land.

Fruit

The lime sulphur spray against big bud on black currants may have burnt the foliage: don't worry too much. It is hoped the scorched foliage will be replaced by fresh growth and that the crop will not suffer too severely. An application of nitro-potash at 1 oz. spread around each bush will help recovery. On an acid or sandy soil, nitro chalk is a wiser choice.

Lawn

The dedicated turfman never puts his mower away, even in the winter.

Narcissus Actaea, a snow-white, sweet-scented poeticus with a marigold eye margined scarlet. An excellent garden plant that may be forced in February.

April
Week 3

Garden flowers

Sow the last of the annuals, thinning out to 2 or 3 ins. apart: those with long tap roots, like the poppies, rarely transplant happily.

Biennials should also be sown, including the sweet williams and wallflowers. The fiery red wallflowers are magnificent, but some of the primrose, rose, lavender and purple varieties deserve to be more seen.

Stake the delphiniums and give the strongest sweet pea shoots a 7 ft. cane.

Violet: whenever I have an interest in a garden I plant the single violet, Princess of Wales, and cannot understand that this irresistible variety is not more grown. This dark violet, single bloom, is exquisite and heavily scented. All the violet asks is a well-decayed leaf-mould and manure compost, and a semi-shaded position. A bank on the north or north-east side of a hedge suits it well. The plant should be kept young and crowns planted now and increased annually by means of runners. Unwanted runners should be dismissed.

If delphinium and lupin cuttings taken earlier (see March – 3rd week) have failed, a second batch can still be planted.

Shrubs

Evergreens can be planted at the latter end of April.

Climbers

We used to be advised to plant clematis at this time, but now they are to be had pot-grown they can be planted with little disturbance at almost any time of the year.

Greenhouse

The temperature may rise to 24°C. (75°F.), and the house should be ventilated early, closing up at teatime. Water in the morning only: plants not in flower will enjoy a syringe with tepid water.

Beware of a dry atmosphere in the greenhouse: it encourages red spider.

Petunias can be sown in a light sandy soil, along with the invaluable winter-flowering primulas, so cheerful in the wintertime and early spring months.

Vegetables

Prepare rich deep trenches for celery and leeks if you are interested in fine specimens.

Onion sets can be planted now.

Make a first sowing of runner beans in deep boxes under glass. These plants make a helpful screen fence if you have a rubbish-heap or an eye-sore to hide.

Main crop potatoes can now be started in the south and west. Whenever frost threatens, potato tips should be lightly covered with soil or straw.

Sow winter cabbage, savoys, broccoli, cauliflowers, and a small pinch of beetroot, and lightly cover with finely sieved soil.

Fruit

Spray against leaf curl and mildew.

Disbud peaches, nectarines, and apricots if they have consented to fruit. Any unwanted buds should be rubbed out.

Watch newly planted fruit trees to see that they do not go dry.

Lawn

As already stressed, from now on the lawn will require regular attention right through the summer.

The first application of fertilizer should be given early this month. Here is a helpful recipe for spring use:

3 parts sulphate of ammonia
3 parts dried blood
4 parts superphosphate
4 parts boneflower
1 part sulphate of potash

Apply when the soil is moist at 2–3 ozs. a sq. yd.

Moss can be controlled by lawn sand, but will inevitably return if the turf is compacted, badly drained, impoverished, or very shady: pipes and a soakway may be necessary if the trouble is not cured by frequent spiking and raking.

Mowing should be more frequent, but blades kept high, not cutting lower than an inch.

Lysichitum Americanum, an exciting spring-flowering water-side plant, with golden trumpets, accompanied by silver-green leaves. It enjoys rich fare and moisture.

April
Week 4

Garden flowers

All garden-flowering chrysanthemums should be planted out during a mild spell. Keep the rows at least 2 ft. apart, so that you can work comfortably among the plants.

Remove the deadheads from the daffodils, but be patient and allow the foliage to die back naturally.

If the dahlia tubers have been kept fairly moist, they should have by now developed small shoots, and can be planted out in mild areas, allowing 2 ft. 6 ins. between all varieties other than poms. Stakes in position first, please!

When the young shoots reach 3–4 ins. they should be thinned out to ground level to encourage stocky plants.

Pick off pansy and viola deadheads, otherwise the plants will stop flowering and concentrate on reproducing themselves by seeding; and watch out for greenfly.

Waterlilies can be planted from now until June. Warning: don't let them dry out while waiting to be planted. They do not require a great depth of water: 18 ins. suits them well.

Make a final planting of pink, red and purple de Caen anemones, richly coloured St. Brigids with fluted petals, Mexican tigridias, the exciting shell flowers, and other summer flowering bulbs. If you live in the south add acidanthera, the white star flower, with a drenching scent, to your list.

Most of the summer-flowering bulbs are rather tender, and benefit by lifting or a good mulch cover before there is danger of frost.

Well hardened-off half-hardies can now be planted out.

Shrubs

Roses: prune back any shoots that have not developed buds, and rub out inward growing and unwanted buds.

Lawn mowings are useful for mulching in the shrubbery, but thick layers of over 2 ins. engender too much heat and are dangerous.

Hedges

Inspect the lately planted hedge: weed, hoe and re-mulch beneath the plants and firm up the soil.

Greenhouse

Plant up the hanging baskets, achimenes, the Hot-water Plant is the easiest of cool greenhouse plants and a splendid basket performer. Place the tuberous roots $\frac{3}{4}$ in. deep and 1 in. apart in John Innes compost. Beware of over-watering in the early stages of growth.

Vegetables

Tomatoes: if they were sown in January, the seedlings will be ready for re-potting or planting in the greenhouse border. Side-growths must be pinched out and the watering can used with care: feeding can be begun once the fruit forms.

Tomatoes can be sown outdoors or young plants ordered. It is difficult to come by the more distinguished varieties and I would advise the gardener to buy Moneymaker, or the good flavoured Elsa Craig seedlings rather than the unnamed, but the more daring among small garden owners might have a go with Sugar Plum, which can be grown in the flower border or in pots on the verandah or in the patio. Stake immediately and tie loosely.

Sow marrows in pots in the greenhouse. Ridge cucumbers can be raised under cloches or in frames.

Complete the planting of brussels sprouts: late plantings are seldom rewarding.

Beetroot: make a small sowing of globe beet.

Sow carrots thinly to avoid thinning out, which encourages carrot fly: soot dressings are an effective fly repellent.

Fruit

Spray or dust the raspberries with derris against the horrid little raspberry beetle that does so much to destroy this delicious fruit. Mildew can be controlled with a colloidal sulphur spray.

Apples should be sprayed with lime sulphur against scab. Spraying should be avoided when flowers are open.

Camomile lawn

I am often asked for my opinion of the camomile lawn. It requires less mowing than turf and is harder wearing: the close plant seems to enjoy the trampling of feet.

Seed should be sown in drills: the tufts transplant well to bare patches where seed has failed. Wiry stalk and unattractive flowers should be dismissed by hand or mower blade. It is, however, possible to obtain plants of the non-flowering form, that will quickly make a lawn.

Triumph tulip Carl M. Bellman, April-flowering, with large blooms and strong stiff stems. The Triumphs fill the gap between the early tulips and the Darwins.

May

The veteran gardener does not trust the month of May – it has treated him too treacherously in the past. But, I love this month: it means lily of the valley and white hawthorn in the country hedges, followed by the honey-scented flowers of the lime, and often a bonus of heavenly days.

The north-westerly wind will dry the soil and a sudden drought may make watering of the newly planted a must.

Meanwhile the late May frost sometimes pays us out for any foolhardy planting. Plants, too, can be caught napping, having responded to a mild spell and hot sunshine.

Planting out from the greenhouse must be done with caution, particularly when the night sky is clear, and protection given to the impatient dahlia or over-eager potatoes and runner beans.

Regular mowing will now become the order of the day. Watering is vital in dry weather and I cannot over-stress the importance of investing in a sprinkler. Maybe in years to come we shall pay more attention to watering our gardens more adequately for we underrate the value of moisture to the plant world.

The battle against rose pests has now started. Combined insecticides and fungicides have lightened the work of spraying, but if the bushes are to be kept clean they must be sprayed every ten days or so. No wonder the rosarian entreats the hybridizer to give him, not finer, but more disease-resistant roses.

Get busy in the herbaceous border, staking, supporting, pinching any leggy growth, thinning out the Michaelmas daisy and delphinium shoots, transplanting, weeding and sowing a few annuals to fill the gaps. Cherry rose nasturtium is a sturdy gap-filler provided you are willing to watch out for blackfly and spray immediately the enemy is spotted. It is almost impossible to dislodge them once established.

Waterlilies and aquatics can be planted from mid-March until June. Make sure your pool is perfectly watertight before starting: a leak will be a constant anxiety. Waterlilies are easier to handle in baskets than just anchored to loam at the base of the pool. Sunrise, a sunny yellow with gold stamens, is a waterlily not to be missed.

Precautionary spraying against blackspot and mildew should begin in earnest.

Delphiniums, lettuce and young growth must be defended against slugs, and the fast growing seedlings of border plants encouraged with a dressing of fertilizer.

All bedding plants and seedlings under glass should be given as much air as possible. But beware of the last May frosts, particularly in the low-lying garden. Meanwhile, a sudden rise of temperature in the greenhouse is also a danger!

Earth up the potatoes and thin out the young crops in the vegetable garden, remembering that at this time of year nature may do some thinning out on its own.

This is a busy month, but time should be found to mulch the fruit trees: they need nourishment and moisture at this stage.

Growing and sowing conditions in the garden are often at their best this month, and, above all, it is lilac time.

Over the years the hybridizer has worked hard on the wishy-washy lilac, *Syringa vulgaris*, and now we have the beautiful, double, white Madame Lemoine (1890), double, red-purple Mrs. Edward Harding, the single, soft primrose-yellow Primrose, and deep purple Souvenir de L. Spath – each more beautiful than the other. Please don't leave out the Canadian hybrids and unique *Syringa* 'Bellicent', with arching plumes of clear pink, tubular flowers.

Among modern and desirable varieties lavender Clarkes' Giant and Blue Hyacinth are outstanding.

Wisteria, cheiranthus and silver tulips.

May
Week 1

Garden flowers

There is no hurry to plant out the bedding plants. If the weather is uncertain, it is quite in order to wait until the end of the month.

Dahlia tubers can be planted out, covered with 2½–3 ins. of soil, but green plants from cuttings must wait until the third week in the south and until June in the north. If you want to plant out earlier than this, cloches or jam jars must be popped on at night. Dwarfs are best planted 16–18 ins. apart for mass effect.

Hardy and half-hardy seed can now be sown in the garden. I believe in sowing in generous drifts, or, on occasion, broadcast: but sowing at stations will be found less confusing by beginners when weeding. I can strongly recommend a sowing of Impatiens, the Patient Lucy. The elfin strain, dwarf and dazzling, does exceptionally well even in the semi-shade.

When the sweet peas reach 9 ins., train the strongest shoot, dismissing all side shoots and tendrils.

Plants are now growing fast: stake and tie regularly, early rather than late.

Unpack plants that have been protected with straw or peat, and cut the ties round the red-hot poker and agapanthus.

Shrubs

Evergreens can still be planted in showery weather and if they are well-watered, mulched and sprayed in drought. But slow-coaches beware, time is now limited.

Prune the ornamental peaches and other spring-flowering shrubs now they have finished flowering.

Keep an eye open for suckers from lilacs and roses, first pushing aside the soil around the sucker to trace its source, and to ensure pulling it away close to its origin. (A growth below the graft is a sucker.)

Greenhouse

I hope the schizanthus is now rewarding you for your care.

Sow cinerarias: they are a boon through the winter, flowering from December to April. The dwarf, large-flowered varieties, often zoned with white at the centre, are outstanding.

Have you picked off the seed pods from the Indian azalea? The plant should not be allowed to waste its energy. Mild doses of fertilizer should be given to ensure strong young growth that will bear next year's flowers.

Go on pricking out the seedlings before they compete for elbow room, and harden off the bedders for planting out.

Vegetables

Thrill! The first asparagus may now be cut, but only from established plants that have been in position for two years.

Tomatoes can be planted in the unheated house. Those in the heated house must be tied in regularly and all side shoots removed.

Celery and leeks should be pricked out. Leeks planted early in the season should now be blanched by slipping brown paper tubes over them. These tubes must be fastened down to bamboo canes and tucked up with soil. This method is time-consuming: the less professional gardener can drop his leeks low on planting and leave it at that.

Marrows can be sown in pots in the greenhouse in cold districts, and in the garden in warm and southern areas.

Winter greens should be planted out when hardened off: the sooner the brussels sprouts and cauliflowers are in their permanent positions, the better.

The main crop beetroot can be sown. A long-rooted variety is advised if the soil is deep and well dug.

Fruit

In northern and cold gardens the strawberry flowers should be protected from late frost with a light covering of straw when frost is imminent. Clean straw beneath the foliage may be needed.

If manure is in short supply, fruit trees can be mulched with spent hops (not to be confused with hop manure that has a chemical content).

Peaches and nectarines should be finally disbudded with discretion.

Apple trees should be sprayed again against scab when reaching 'pink bud stage'.

Lawn

The lawn should be mown at least once a week, lowering the blades to three-quarters of an inch.

Go on lightly aerating and raking out dead moss only.

Fritillaria imperialis, the snake's head fritillary, with graceful hanging heads and slender stems. They seed themselves and naturalize happily in the grass.

May
Week 2

Garden flowers

It is getting late to sow half-hardies outdoors, and possible that an early autumn frost may cut their life short. However, you should get some welcome September bloom when the earlier sown are fading out. Ten-week stocks should not be forgotten, and *Convolvulus major* always gives a good show.

Don't forget to pinch out the tendrils on the sweet peas to induce the sap into the growing point. If early flowers form they should also be dismissed: flowering must not be allowed until four blooms mature on each stem.

If the ground was well prepared, regular feeding will not be necessary, but the plants must not be allowed to dry out and a drink of liquid manure or soot water followed by a mulch of well-rotted compost will not come amiss.

Manure water is made by hanging a small sack of well-rotted manure to soak in a bucket or container of water. It should be left until the liquid becomes straw or tea-coloured.

If there are budding gardeners in the family, a packet of a children's collection of seeds, including the foolproof marigolds, candytuft, cornflowers, radishes, mustard and cress, and carrots, is worth sowing.

Chrysanthemums: Earlies should be planted out this week: they look well, spaced 18 ins. apart, in triangular groups of three. Keep the ground around them hoed, and the soil surface open and free of weeds. The plant should not be allowed more than six blooms if you want size and quality.

Indoor plants

House plants will enjoy a blow in the garden, but should be brought in at night. Cuttings of many house plants, among them the tradescantia, aphelandra and ficus, can be taken.

If you want the 'trad' to develop pink-shaded foliage, it must be given a sunny position.

Shrubs

Complete heather pruning, carrying out heavy trimming with shears.

Mulch rhododendrons and azaleas with peat or leaf-soil when the soil is moist.

Plant out any young shrubs and trees, such as the *Arbutus unedo*, the Killarney strawberry tree, with bunches of creamy bells and orange fruit that arrive almost simultaneously. Young pot plants are to be had of this attractive dark green, evergreen shrub, that given time, becomes a tree.

Greenhouse

Other than in the very cold district, the more tender of the half-hardies, such as the morning glories and zinnias can be put outdoors.

Vegetables

Dwarf French beans can be sown in many gardens.

Thin the turnips drastically.

Support the peas when they have reached 6–9 ins.

Sow runner beans in the south, waiting until the end of the month in the north. (A few may be sown under glass for planting out in late May or early June.)

Thin the onions and dust against flea beetle.

Black-flies continue to put in an appearance this month. Spray on sight with a weak insecticide.

Herbs

Sow more parsley: there isn't a more useful herb.

Fruit

Reduce the number of young raspberry growths to the number required for next year's fruiting canes.

Stop the growth of vines at two or three leaves beyond the bunch. These shoots should be tied firmly to the wires and the tips kept from touching the glass.

Thin out old wood on the gooseberries: weak and crossing branches in the centre of the plant should also go.

Lawn

Mowings from lawns recently treated with selective weedkiller must not be used for mulching.

Clematis Bees Jubilee, in shades of pink and carmen on a white ground: a free and vigorous grower.

May
Week 3

Garden flowers

A late planting of summer-flowering bulbs is possible in gardens well protected from autumn winds.

Biennials can be sown: double daisies, Canterbury bells, foxgloves, forget-me-nots, honesty, sweet williams and wall-flowers.

If there is a flower-arranger in the family, a packet-collection of flowers chosen for this specific purpose, that includes summer and dried winter decorations, should be sown.

Tulips and daffodils that are now faded can be lifted, any remaining deadheads removed and the bulbs heeled in shallow drills in the vegetable garden.

Tie or push back the untidy *Iris unguicularis* foliage so that the sun can bake the roots.

Many of the primula family, primrose, polyanthus, auricula, *P. denticulata* and Wanda can be lifted and divided after flowering. The best strains should be marked when in flower for propagation later.

Indoor plants

Christmas cactus can be propagated by detaching two segments and inserting them in a sandy compost at the side of a pot. Christmas Joy, a splendid flame-coloured hybrid recently introduced from Germany, has given a wonderful display on my office window-sill in spite of interference from the cleaner's duster.

Calceolarias can be sown now. This comic plant with its brilliant pouches is not one of my favourites and seldom gets a write-up from me. But no doubt it has its fans, and I must confess, the latest giant strains in yellow, orange and scarlet 'tigered' and spotted in contrasting colours, are very dashing.

Shrubs

Grafted lilacs have a maddening habit of suckering: a mulch of grass mowings discourages these tiresome shoots that considerably weaken the plant.

Treat the roses to a fertilizer, strictly according to the manufacturer's directions.

Greenhouse

Cyclamen can now go out to the cool, shaded frame.

Pot on the rooted geranium and fuchsia cuttings, and take more if wanted.

Chrysanthemums: the final potting of Large Exhibition, Exhibition Incurved, Decoratives and Singles into 8, 9 or 10 in. pots should be undertaken, using John Innes Potting Compost No. 1 or a chrysanthemum compost. Once potted, the plants can be stood on a hard, not soil, surface in rows in the open. Space should be left in the pots for top-dressing.

Vegetables

I would like to stress the value of the easy-going Kohl-rabi, particularly to gardeners who have been unsuccessful with parsnips. It is a biennial that makes a useful catch-crop, and thinnings can be easily transplanted.

Runner beans can be planted out in warm gardens.

A batch of runner beans for seed-saving should be sown at the end of the rows.

Find a warm spot for the outdoor tomatoes, against a wall, facing south if possible.

Herbs

Plant a packet of *bouquet garni* on fertile ground for the enthusiastic cook.

Fruit

The vine: a warm temperature must be maintained when the flowers open to assist the drying of pollen so that it can be passed from bloom to bloom. Pollination should be carried out at midday, allowing the bunch of bloom to pass lightly through your hand, coating your palm with pollen before your hand travels on to the next bunch.

Lawn

Weed killing must now begin in earnest, using lawn sand or, perhaps, a selective hormone killer. A dry, warm, windless morning, with rain in the offing, is the perfect day for such an application, but if lawn sand is used and there is no rainfall after two to three days, it must be watered in. Keep a watch particularly on sunny days for any scorching.

The manufacturer's instructions should be followed to the letter: otherwise there is the danger that the turf may be burnt black-brown, a condition that disturbs the most level-headed of gardeners.

Beware of letting the lawn dry out, and a reminder that dribs and drabs do more harm than good. Give the turf a good soak and allow it to partly dry out before soaking it again.

If the lawn looks starved, an early summer compound fertilizer may be called for: otherwise a spring and autumn dressing should fill the bill.

A raised and familiar rock planting of aubrieta, alyssum saxatile and potentillas, the rock roses.

May
Week 4

Garden flowers

Chelsea, the most important flower show in the world, to which two hundred thousand people make a gardening pilgrimage, takes place about the fourth week in May.

The show ground, covering twenty-three acres, belongs to the Royal Chelsea Hospital, where veteran soldiers may spend their last days. They are watched with respect and affection as in their bright scarlet coats they bend on their sticks in order to poke their noses into sweetly scented roses.

The standard of plants and flowers is high, and nurserymen use all their skill to keep the early spring flowers back until late May by means of the refrigerator. The tulips will have been hurried on or delayed, according to their variety and the weather.

Almost every plant is represented, from Patient Lucy and the Wandering Jew to the most distinguished orchid.

There are also entries from Continental growers that help to replace the gigantic displays by our own seedsmen, Suttons, Carters and Unwins who have withdrawn due to the heavy and mounting expense.

Chelsea will always be Chelsea, where there is much to be learned and admired: it is an occasion a gardener cannot afford to miss.

Now back to the week's work.

All bedding plants should now be in place. When planting edgings, have a care to keep the plants a reasonable distance from the turf and the blades of the mowing machine.

Sweet peas will now be growing by the inch daily: side shoots and tendrils must be pinched out and early flower buds too if good sized blooms are wanted later on.

Cut back the lupin stems and deadhead the pansies and violas.

Pyrethrums can now be cut down, and divided, or planted.

Indoor plants

Exacum affine is a pleasant, small plant easily grown from seed indoors, and useful as a summer house plant.

Shrubs

Remove seed pods from the rhododendrons and do not allow any of the spring flowering shrubs to waste their energy on seeding.

Make sure the newly planted wall shrubs do not go thirsty.

Watch out for suckers from grafted lilacs and roses, and tear them away at their point of origin.

Summer-flowering shrubs, among them the weigela and mock-orange, may be pruned after flowering.

Disbud the hybrid tea roses.

Continue to spray the roses to control mildew, blackspot and insects before pest and disease establish themselves. Regular attention pays.

Climbers

Feed the climbing roses generously with fertilizer and tie them in as they grow.

Greenhouse

Provide shade for plants in flower and damp down staging and floor daily to provide humidity.

Begonias and gloxinias sown at the beginning of the year will now call for 3–3½ in. pots.

If more hydrangeas are wanted for next year, hurry up and take cuttings.

Vegetables

Top-dress the cucumbers in the greenhouse regularly when their roots poke through the soil.

Keep up the supply of lettuce by successional sowing.

Chicory should be sown and thinned to 1 ft. apart. Should flower buds appear later on, they must be removed.

Have you sown cabbages and savoys in the nursery bed for use next year?

Ridge cucumbers raised in the greenhouse can be planted out.

Fruit

Cut out any young raspberry canes that are crowding the centre of the plant.

Melons form at the first leaf joint: side shoots can be trained to grow outwards and should be tied to supports.

Spray apples at petal fall and fruitlet stage as a final precaution against apple scab: currants should also be sprayed against fly and spider, and black currants with lime sulphur against big bud. A nicotine or derris spray is valuable just now as capsid bugs do much damage to currants and gooseberries as well as to many ornamental subjects.

Red spider on peaches and nectarines can be prevented by regular syringing with soft water and routine spraying with derris or pyrethrum.

Meconopsis sheldoni, the beautiful but temperamental blue poppy, that has no liking for lime and prefers the semi-shade.

June

We seldom get a flaming June, but the sun will be at its strongest, and this is often the driest month of the year.

Temperatures rise from time to time to 27°C. (81°F.) in the afternoons, but unfortunately thunderstorms have the habit of abruptly ending the fine summer spells.

Roses are said to be the epitome of June but the month is surely shared with the cottager's paeony. I like the way when picked their massive heads disintegrate on the table with a loud bang when their day is done.

Watering becomes more demanding and those who have not been able to mulch the newly planted will have to work overtime with the hose once the sun has gone down.

Weeds too will grow apace: it pays to keep the hoe moving. Paraquat and other effective weed-killers lighten the work of the modern gardener.

Staking is essential: a sudden storm can play havoc in the border and ruin a year's

July

July does not always have the highest temperatures and the hottest days of the year. We can generally count on some very hot days in the Home Counties, but the fine weather soon breaks up with a thunderstorm accompanied by merciless rain or hail. Westerly winds may lead to July being one of the wettest months of the year.

Plants transpire freely, and unless there is rainfall will suffer if not mulched or watered.

Should drought persist, any autumn- or spring-planted shrub looking crestfallen in the heat should be treated to an evening syringe of water.

Keep your evergreen hedge nicely trimmed. Should you fancy trying your hand at topiary, clip a couple of yews in pyramid or corkscrew designs to stand in tubs at either side of your front door. Topiary is a slow and ticklish job, but a fascinating pastime.

Meanwhile, the flower garden should, in theory, be a riot of colour. You may not catch up with your summer border dream but if you haven't some colour in your garden at this time of year – then your fingers are not green.

Deadheading must be done daily, otherwise plants will lose their interest in flowering and put all their energy into seeding.

 July
Week 4

Garden flowers

Sow annual carnations in the border or over-winter and flower there next year.

the white, grey, grey-green and pale

given, I hope, its usual splendid performance, will now need a rest in a cool place, water being almost entirely withheld.

A successful octogenarian grower advised me to wait for the hippeastrum to break the pot before re-potting. His way of saying only repot when you have to.

August

August weather usually follows the same pattern as that of July: the atmospheric conditions are often similar and the two months add up to a fine or wet summer.

Although autumn has not yet shown sign of taking over, plants and trees have, alas, lost their youth, and many are overgrown and blowsy.

If rainfall is low, regular watering will be called for, but the heavy dews will help to replace plant transpiration.

Many gardeners will be taking a holiday this month: maybe there is a neighbour who can pick and enjoy your flowers and perishable fruit while you are on holiday?

If not, pick as many flowers as you can before you go, buds and all, so that seed pods are not formed in your absence.

Up with as many dandelions and plantains before you leave: given the chance they multiply more generously than rabbits.

Ties and stakes should be examined: don't leave your treasured plants at the mercy of a storm.

The roses should be given a last spray against aphis, blackspot and mildew, and if the earwigs are tormenting the dahlias, lure as many of them as you can into an upturned, straw-lined pot and drown them.

Gardeners staying at home will find plenty of jobs going begging.

It is an excellent month to sow a new lawn. Warm August soil is perfect for fast germination.

I am no liker of concrete or crazy paving, but I understand concrete paths are useful, and August is a good time to put one down.

Now that the greenhouse is cleared of bedding-plants, and those that enjoy a summer blow in the garden, it is an admirable moment to paint and repair.

The heating system and soil warming cables should be checked, and electric power inspected by a local authority: this is not only a safe precaution, but usually cheaper in the end.

Should August hang heavily on the gardener's hands he might consider laying the foundation for a pool or rock garden, but now he has the right to lie back in a comfortable garden chair, and reap the reward of his labour.

Meanwhile, the gardener on holiday will be visiting horticultural and private gardens, nurseries, and garden centres thrown in, with it is hoped, notebook in hand.

I would suggest he looks out for the lovely *Alstromeria ligtu* hybrids in pink, coral, yellow and buff that flower through July and early August: these are not easy customers, but thoroughly worth cosseting: the new huge hibiscus from Japan, 'Southern Belle', should not be difficult to track down, and the exciting, but rather tender, fuchsias from America must not be missed.

Other plants worth finding are the dignified *eremurus* or foxtail lily, the *Magnolia grandiflora*, the unique evergreen of the family, presenting its immense sweet-scented flowers just now, and *Romneya coulteri*, the Californian poppy, with grey-green foliage and petals of white, crinkled paper, that surround a golden centre.

Well-planted annual and perennial borders, that, even if past their best, still hold a load of beauty, and different flower associations are always worth attention.

On coming home, you may find the old-fashioned roses in full bloom to greet you, and the white and mauve Japanese anemones may have taken charge, giving the autumn garden a fresh look.

How good to eat your own fresh vegetables again! – cut younger, smaller and fresher by your hand than any other. And autumn strawberries, Giant Grandee and Gento, waiting to be picked . . . A gardener's welcome.

Kniphofia 'Springtime'.

August
Week 1

Garden flowers

Many a gardener takes his hols. in August, but goes away with certain foreboding. Will there be a drought in his absence? To whom can he entrust his blue poppies and the lilies that are the apple of his eye?

Early chrysanthemums will now be coming into bloom and must be protected against wind and rain. Greaseproof bags should be used to cover blooms that are intended for a flower show.

Take cuttings of geraniums, Washington pelargoniums (the Regals), penstemons and calceolarias.

Check the ties and stake the heavy foliaged perennials in the border.

The wayward Madonna lily, with its preference for cottage gardens, should be planted in batches. Sit them on small cushions of sand. Sun is essential to this lily.

Hardy annuals can be sown in the border to over-winter: some of the finest larkspurs can be raised this way.

If the sweet pea bed was well prepared, it should not be necessary to feed the plants, but they must not be allowed to go dry. Sweet pea fans may care to spray with water at the end of a hot day, or 'straw' the paths between the rows, keeping the latter wet to increase humidity so that the foliage and stems remain soft and sappy.

I always associate the nostalgic scent of white phlox with a hot night in August. This flower has the very special charm of shining out in the darkness. Make a note in your diary to plant the excellent variety, 'White Admiral', when autumn comes.

Indoor plants

Achimenes, that have given of their best, should now be gradually dried off.

Shrubs

Go ahead propagating your favourite shrubs.

More hydrangea cuttings may be taken if required. They sell well at charity bazaars.

Lavender cuttings, 4–6 ins. long, can be struck outdoors this month: remove the lowest leaves from the stems and insert the cuttings close to each other for protection to a depth of two-thirds of their length.

Hedges

Clip lonicera nitida and cupressus hedges now. If clipping is left until autumn, the tender young growth that results has no time to ripen before the early frosts and will suffer.

Greenhouse

Pansy and fuchsia cuttings strike well in a frame, and can be propagated now.

Stalwart antirrhinums are to be had for next year by sowing now in a temperature of 15°C. (59°F.).

Gardeners who prefer growing freesia corms to raising seed, should plant now: 6–8 corms to a 5 in. pot, covering them with $\frac{1}{2}$ in. of soil, afterwards placing the pots in a frame. The soil used should be nicely moist, making it unnecessary to water until the corms start growing.

Vegetables

Spray potatoes again as a protection against blight.

Sow winter lettuce.

Examine celery for fly.

Sow brussels for transplanting in the spring.

Endives can be blanched by placing a flower pot over the plant (covering the drainage hole at the bottom of the pot with a piece of tile or a flat stone). Blanching checks growth and should not be started until the plant has reached a reasonable height.

Pickling onions can also be lifted, laid on the ground to ripen, dried off and picked without delay. The thick neck should be checked in growth by bending over.

Fruit

Early apples should be eaten as soon as possible. They won't keep.

Have you cut out the unwanted raspberry and loganberry canes after fruiting?

Shorten the lush growth on the plums.

Wall trees that are looking dry should be given a thorough soaking, but peaches and nectarines now fruiting should be fed and watered with discretion.

Place a small piece of wood behind peaches and nectarines growing against a wall, to expose them to the sun, and remove a few leaves, if necessary.

Many of the strawberry runners can now be separated from the parent plant.

Get rid of the wasps. Study their flight and track them down: only the experienced hand should attempt to destroy the nest.

Lawn

A sprinkling of nitro-potash dissolved in water is a splendid stimulant for a tired lawn, and, as a reader described it to me, 'a super bit of advice'.

Water-lily 'Escarboucle', a large crimson flower and one of the best of the reds.

August
Week 2

Garden flowers

Autumn-flowering crocus, ordered earlier, should be planted as soon as they arrive as they have a habit of rushing into flower.

If you have an orchard or wild garden where their lilac cups can spread themselves, a drift of colchicums (a size or two larger than the crocus and rather more showy) should be added.

Have you tried the everlasting flowers and ornamental grasses? They should be cut just before they reach their zenith, on a sunny day when the dew has dried.

Helichrysum should be picked before the central boss of the flower discloses itself, and heads sans stems should be laid out on newspaper to dry. Stems do not lend themselves to drying, but heads are easily mounted on wires.

Dried flowers, with strong stems, should be hung up in small bunches so that the air can get to each bloom: they must be defended from direct sunshine.

Flowers can be dried in the airing cupboard, but the natural way is gentler and kinder.

The bouquets must be stored in a dry atmosphere: they will deteriorate rapidly in a damp or dusty place.

Preserving is seldom completely successful: succulents should not be attempted and all subjects becoming dangerously brittle must be handled with a fairylike touch.

Stachys lanata, or Lambs' ears, respond quite well to drying and make a delightful surround to a Victorian posy of ever-lastings.

Keep your eye on the dahlias for sickly and mottled growth that denotes the presence of virus. Affected plants should be lifted and burnt.

Have you pricked out the June-sown wallflowers, forget-me-nots and polys? They should soon be ready to move to the nursery bed: they can then be planted in their permanent positions in October.

Baskets, tubs and window-boxes deserve a taste of a reputable pep-up fertilizer to keep them blooming until the frost. Regular and thorough watering is a must.

Shrubs

Be sure to step up your spraying of roses against black spot, that becomes more virulent from now onwards.

Summer-flowering shrubs, among them the weigela and mock orange, may be pruned after flowering.

Greenhouse

Keep the greenhouse well-ventilated: a muggy atmosphere encourages mildew.

Prepared hyacinths for Christmas flowering should be ordered from a bulb specialist. They are likely to be a little more pricey, but they are worth every penny. They seldom fail.

The heavily scented Paper White and Soleil d'Or narcissus should also be planted early.

Perhaps I should point out to the beginner that tulips are less reliable as pot plants than the hyacinth and daffodil.

Beauty of Nice stocks can be sown now and make delightful pot plants in the spring.

Vegetables

Watch tomatoes for whitefly: if the fly persists, the greenhouse must be fumigated.

Make a first sowing of spring cabbage.

Earth up leeks and celery, week by week.

Beetroot often grows coarse at this time of year and is best lifted young, stored and covered with a suspicion of soil.

Keep peas and beans regularly watered and mulched.

Fruit

Harden your heart and give the fruit a final thinning. This not only leads to larger fruit, but encourages regular cropping, giving the trees the opportunity of building up fruit buds for next year. Over-cropping often results in a tree getting into the undesirable habit of 'alternate year' cropping.

Silver leaf disease is infectious during the late summer, autumn and winter, and pruning must wait until next spring when the risk of infection is reduced by the sap barrier that follows spring pruning.

Lawn

Weeds should not be allowed to establish themselves, and a final selective weedkiller application may now be given.

Magnolia grandiflora, the evergreen species with noble cream flowers of heavy fragrance, measuring as much as 10 in. across.

August
Week 3

Garden flowers

The asters or Michaelmas daisies, with their many new varieties and widened colour range, are an important family, that keep the autumn garden gay. But they have one ghastly failing: no plant is more vulnerable to mildew. Unless sprayed early before the powdery disease is established, it is impossible to keep it at bay. It is a menace in a damp season.

Have you disbudded the outdoor chrysanthemums? Japs will soon need similar attention.

Sever stems of layered carnations, but wait to lift them until next month.

Take cuttings of violas and violets.

Foliage

Various types of foliage can be preserved in glycerine this month and afterwards used for winter decoration.

The glycerine should be diluted with hot water that has been brought to the boil: (1 part glycerine to 2 parts hot (boiled) water).

The leaves should be immaculate and unmarked by aphis or disease.

After gathering, stems should be split and stood in warm water overnight. They should then be placed in a jar with a depth of 2–3 ins. of the diluted glycerine.

The gardener must now wait until the foliage shows signs that the glycerine has reached the veins of the leaves. This will take anything between 3 days and 3 weeks. (Beech 3 weeks, laurel 3 days.)

The stems should not be left standing in the glycerine longer than necessary. The liquid can be saved and used again.

Beech, laurel, aspidistra and magnolia lend themselves particularly well to this sort of treatment.

Indoor plants

Take cuttings of *Campanula isophylla :* place the cuttings round the side of a pot and allow them to grow together as one plant.

Shrubs

Plants often droop through dryness at this time of year. A good soak must be given: dribs and drabs merely bring roots to the hot and dry surface soil.

The benefits of mulching cannot be overstressed, sending the roots downwards in search of moisture.

Almost all evergreen clippings will happily serve as cuttings.

Lavender can be trimmed after flowering.
Remove rose suckers.

Greenhouse

Heliotrope (cherry pie) cuttings can now be taken.

Arum lilies may be stirred into growth after a summer rest.

Cyclamen should be brought in from the frame: plants may be raised from seed sown now.

Pot on the cinerarias, calceolarias, primulas and others that are pot-bound.

Greenhouse peaches need constant ventilation: otherwise botrytis will develop at the union of stem and fruit, due to moisture.

Vegetables

Lift onions grown from sets.

Dust celery with soot. Some gardeners prefer to sprinkle the soil with salt and contend it keeps the sticks crisp.

Dig up potatoes when skins are 'set'. (Test this with a light rub of the thumb.)

Herbs

Cut down the mint and top-dress with peat and compost to encourage young growth.

Earth up and re-plant chives if overcrowded.

Fruit

Remove any old dark-coloured wood that has borne fruit from the blackcurrants and keep the centre of the gooseberry bushes open by shortening young side growths to three buds (if protected from finches).

Watch the grapes for mildew and cut out affected berries before they spoil the bunch.

Prune the morello cherry by removing as much as possible of the old fruiting wood as soon as the fruit is picked.

Birds

Summer is ending, and the cuckoo may have already said good-bye.

Other birds are rounding up in the sky and huddling together at night-time as if to get to know each other better and gain courage from company before making the long and dangerous flight to the south.

A tight planting of begonias semperflorens, Southbank hybrids, along with cineraria maritima 'White Diamond'.

August
Week 4

Garden flowers

Last cuttings can be taken from the bedding geraniums, planting them in some sheltered corner and treating them to a generous dollop of sharp sand.

Stake the Michaelmas daisies that are now heavy with bloom against wind and rains; and dust with sulphur to control mildew.

I never tire of recommending the winter and spring-flowering crocus species that should be ordered now: they are real jewels and far more precious than their large globular Dutch relations. Tomasinianus, with small flowers of silver lilac, and Gipsy Girl of shining butter-gold (the petals are feathered chocolate brown on the outside) should not be missed.

Trim back the violas and treat them to a tasty top-dressing.

Indoor plants

Office plant: this is the time to take Busy Lizzie or Patient Lucy cuttings, rooting them either in water or soil.

Shrubs

Control mildew on ornamental crabs, shrub roses and climbers with karathane spray.

Cuttings of shrubs can still be taken by pulling away side shoots with a heel of old wood attached.

Order shrubs for autumn planting.

Try your hand at layering a magnolia or species clematis that presents low growing branches.

Climbers

Tie in the rambler roses that have made new growth since pruning.

Greenhouse

The sweetest flower I know, and my favourite in the spring bulb parade, is the white Roman hyacinth. It should be ordered now as it sells fast and is not in abundant supply.

Fresh and innocent, it flowers from November onwards, its far-reaching, ravishing scent leads us into thinking that spring is round the corner.

Fuchsia cuttings taken now should be grown on through the winter.

When the gloxinias fade they should be gradually dried off and stored undisturbed in their pots in a temperature not lower than 10°C. (50°F.). The corms must be allowed to rest through the winter and may be wakened up in February.

Geraniums and Regal pelargonium cuttings, young heather shoots and shrub cuttings may also be inserted for rooting now.

Vegetables

When the sweet corn tassels show signs of wear and withering, and the corn exudes a milky substance when gently pressed with your thumb-nail, the cob is ready for picking.

Outdoor tomatoes can be hurried in ripening by untying them and laying them on a straw bed under cloches.

Re-mulch the peas and beans and water them regularly in drought to keep the plants cropping.

Go ahead earthing up the celery.

Fruit

Early maturing varieties of apples and pears are better picked before fully ripe.

To test for ripeness, lift and gently twist the fruit, when, if ready for picking, it will part from the spur.

Protect your show fruit from wasps.

Lawn

Weeds, such as clover, yarrow or Yorkshire fog, must not be allowed to establish themselves.

If a new lawn is to be sown, careful preparations must be made, and a reputable fertilizer applied to the soil. The seed should be ready to hand.

The modern seedsman offers a series of mixtures, and it is for the gardener to decide what kind of lawn he wants.

Is it to be the slow-growing, velvet show-lawn that we all dream about? Or a superfine grass for the tennis player? Among other blends are the 'general purpose' for hard wear, the 'play lawn' that survives children, dogs and what have you, and the 'tough grass' mixture that has no look or pretence of velvet, but gives maximum wear for minimum cost.

General

Garden waste should be collected for sandwiching with layers of kitchen waste, grass mowings, wood ash and soot, etc. Thick 'bodge' layers should be avoided and a sprinkling of sulphate of ammonia added, or one of the many proprietary products, to hasten decomposition.

Another compost heap should be started.

Collerette dahlia 'Nonsense' is white with a becoming pink collar. It looks well planted along with lilac white-collared Can Can.

September

The Michaelmas daisies and the Japanese anemones are still giving a lavish display, but the annuals are almost played out, and the days are visibly shortening.

The China asters do their best to hold attention, and the single daisy-like and button varieties have a certain charm.

The important planting months, October and November, are approaching, and trees, shrubs and plants must be ordered so that they can be planted while the soil is warm.

The gardener with a family and a wish to be remembered, can do no better than plant a tree. Many gardeners must regret that their parents did not plant an oak, lime, or even a maple or magnolia to commemorate their birth.

The choice is legion, but I would like to suggest the planting of a Georgian favourite, the pear. Walking through St. John's Wood, N.W.1. last spring, I found the pears in full flood of blossom, and here and there an octogenarian mulberry made its mark.

I planted a golden catalpa in Holland Park when I married. The golden variety is rather scarce and my tree is now among the tallest of its kind in central London. The catalpa is too upright in habit to present shade, but it has a noble bearing, large, impressive leaves, and is a telling colour.

If space does not allow for a tree, then a shrub must be chosen. For those on acid soil it may be a camellia 'Donation', a striking Himalayan rhododendron, or the prized arbutus (strawberry tree). For a small garden, a sweet-scented *Azalea japonica* is ideal.

Robinia frisia, one of the false acacias, is the fashionable tree as I write: its bright yellow-green, finely designed foliage has taken gardeners by storm.

I would like to recommend the aromatic rosemary to the friendly gardener who enjoys giving cuttings away. This romantic plant with a host of sentimental connections, can be passed on to friends and lovers by a sprig (a half-ripened young shoot), in August or September. The rosemary is an accommodating plant that thrives in a light soil.

Preparation for planting entails digging and forking a deep generous hole, as much as $1\frac{1}{2}$–2 ft. square.

The soil mixture of garden compost, peat and well-rotted manure, must be ready and handy to line the hole and dribble in between the roots.

Other significant work this month is the potting up of 'prepared' bulbs in the home and greenhouse, the planting of daffodils, snowdrops and other early-flowering bulbs in the beds and borders or in the grass if there is a wild garden, adding perhaps a few of the brilliant tulip species that do not require autumn lifting and increase so well if left undisturbed.

Soil from the compost heap, with a dusting of bonemeal, suits the bulbs far better than manure.

The vegetable plot should be kept clear of decaying foliage from maturing green crops, the potatoes lifted and the carrots stored when ready.

If new fruit trees are to be planted, the ground should be prepared for them, while apples and pears should be harvested when ready.

Autumn is the time to carry out any repairs to the lawn, levelling up hollows with sprinklings of finely sieved compost and rolling back the turf and flattening out the bumps. The mower blades may be slightly raised from now onwards, and spiking with a fork will improve drainage where the turf is over-compacted.

September can offer some of the loveliest days of the year and perfect moonlight nights.

Asters: the Michaelmas daisies.

September
Week 1

Garden flowers

The roses now burst into their second flush, the dahlias are heavy with bloom while golden rod and Michaelmas daisies, hungry trespassers, take over the neglected go-as-you-please garden.

Michaelmas daisies, heavy with bloom, may need extra support.

Sweet pea lovers can start a new cycle by sowing in the open ground late this month, afterwards covering the seedlings with cloches. Once they are established, protection will only be needed in severe weather, but mice and slugs may well be troublesome.

The gardener should be rewarded for his trouble and early sowing by exceptionally fine blooms next year.

Don't let any faded spikes of flowers spoil the look of the border.

Keep the dahlias flowering by removing deadheads.

Indoor plants

Once the spring bulbs are potted they are best plunged outdoors under a north wall, either buried in soil or covered with sand and ashes.

Shrubs

Protect the tender shrub or plant against an early freakish frost: bracken or straw are effective protection.

September is a good month for planting evergreens.

Rose cuttings can be taken of ripe shoots of early summer's growth. The base of the cuttings should be dipped first in water and then in a rooting hormone powder to a depth of at least 1 in. A sheltered place not overhung by trees should be found and a trench dug and sprinkled with coarse sand. The cuttings should be placed in this trench with about one-third of their length above the ground. Fill in the soil and gently tread in so that the cuttings are upright.

Any new roses should be ordered.

Greenhouse

Lilies usually at their best in July and August, are a sumptuous joy if brought into the house. They should be returned to the greenhouse after flowering.

Tomatoes must make way for chrysanthemums. The tomatoes can be ripened in the house.

Cyclamen must be brought from the frame into a cool, airy greenhouse before danger of frost.

Gloxinias and tuberous begonias should be examined regularly while drying off.

Late chrysanthemums should be treated to a feed once the buds have set.

Perpetual carnations and indoor chrysanthemums should now be safe in the greenhouse. The chrysanthemums should be sprayed against pest and mildew.

Vegetables

Sow early-maturing carrots, cauliflowers, lettuce, onions and winter spinach.

Carrots are best lifted early: left in the ground they are apt to split.

Onions store well if roped, and where space is short, can then be hung under the eaves of a frostproof shed. Start by tying a large onion at the bottom of a strong cord, and then build up by tying on more onions until the cord is filled up.

Haricot beans can be pulled up when dry and hung up under cover in a cool, airy place: they can be shelled when dry.

Main crop potatoes, if grown, should be lifted. They will not grow any larger and are vulnerable to disease and pest (in particular the slug) while in the soil. The beginner may have been warned that he should not lift until the tuber skin rubs off with pressure from his thumb. Let him turn a deaf ear!

Some gardeners harvest tomatoes when pink and let them finish ripening indoors: this enables the plant to put its energy into the fruit left growing.

Fruit

The store should be made clean and ready for the final harvesting of crops. Hay should not be used for bedding as it taints the fruit. An over-dry atmosphere can be avoided by damping the floor.

If grape bunches are surrounded by heavy foliage, a few leaves may be pushed aside, or removed, to admit the sun.

Lace-cap hydrangeas 'Blue Wave' with fertile flowers surrounded by large white bracts. A splendid ground cover shrub.

September
Week 2

Garden flowers

Clean up the rock garden and the surprising debris that surrounds the plants, and top-dress the plants with finely sieved leaf-mould and grit.

Iris unguicularis can be planted or transplanted. Roots must be kept moist until established.

When planting spring bulbs do not forget the *Leucojum vernum*, the spring snowflake, with petals tipped with green. Left undisturbed it will multiply.

Groom the pick of the hardy chrysanthemums and earlies before taking them into the greenhouse.

Short side shoots of perennials, previously cut down, may be detached and are easily rooted.

A further planting of freesias may be made: they thrive in warmth, but resent forcing. If the pots can be brought inside from the frame in batches their performance will be prolonged.

Give the chrysanthemums plenty of ventilation and water in the morning only. Beware of an uneven day and night temperature that leads to damping off.

Vegetables

Cabbages should not be fed or manured now or they will make soft growth that will not survive the winter. If they are growing too close, alternate plants can be sent to the kitchen in the spring.

Sow a last row of kale: it is a great winter standby.

If late marrows, squashes and pumpkins are slow in ripening and still on the plants, they should be raised on glass or wood

September
Week 3

Garden flowers

The best of the hardy chrysanthemums intended for propagation later on should be labelled with tie-ons.

Border carnations layered in July and now rooted, may be separated from the parent plant.

New beds or borders that are to be made should be dug now.

The seedsman will soon be bombarding the gardener with catalogues, describing new and startling introductions that make excellent reading. (Some have to be bought these days.)

When making your order, a sprinkling of newcomers should be included as a fillip to the well-tried varieties that have proved themselves.

Shrubs

Shrub cuttings will root readily in a cold frame or sheltered shrubbery.

Conifers transplant well this month. Gardeners faced with an ugly structure or seeking privacy from neighbours, should plant *Cupressocyparis leylandii:* this columnar evergreen is the fastest grower we possess and will quickly act as a screen and defence.

When moving larger plants such as conifers and evergreens, reduce the shock by preparing for lifting: this can be done by driving a spade deep down at two sides of the plant (doing the same to the two other sides a fortnight later). This will sever large roots and lead to the plant forming fibrous roots.

Greenhouse

Pot up a few gay polyanthus and place them in a frame or greenhouse for early flowering.

Geraniums, fuchsias, begonias, heliotropes and tender subjects should now be in the greenhouse, and cyclamen and primulas brought in from the frame.

Geranium and fuchsia cuttings must be examined regularly for grey mould and any sufferer dismissed.

Outside chrysanthemums should be housed without delay.

Sweet peas under glass are something of a luxury. They should be sown in September (4 seeds to a 5 in. pot): when potted on in January they can be plunged up to the rim in the greenhouse

border. A steady temperature of 17°C (63°F.) should be maintained: a high temperature, even for an hour, might prove fatal.

As winter approaches the thought of possessing a greenhouse becomes more attractive. My advice to the gardener is not to buy a cheap one.

Look around and, with the help of a knowledgeable adviser, test the various houses for light, ventilation, temperature, humidity and deterioration.

Experience tells me that it is seldom worthwhile building your own greenhouse: even if you are a do-it-yourself man, the cost is almost as great, and there is no comeback if things go wrong.

Vegetables

This is harvest time: go ahead with the storing, clearing the ground as you go. Keep the crops gathered just before they reach their prime and do not allow the plants to put their energy into ripening seed.

Lettuce of a suitable variety can be grown in a frame for winter use. Successional sowings will keep the supply going.

This is one of the best months for 'spawning' (sowing) mushrooms under cover, in a frame or shed. They will crop in about six weeks and follow on those grown outdoors.

Fruit

A new bed of strawberries may be made this month. New, certified virus-free stock should be bought from a reputable source. Planting should be completed by the end of the month.

Make sure all grape bunches are getting enough sun. (See September, 1st week).

Lawn

Puff balls and fairy rings have a habit of appearing at this time of year. When brushed away they may leave a tell-tale green circle and later a thin line of bare earth.

The ring should be deeply spiked with a tine fork and well soaked with a solution of 2 oz. of Epsom salts to the gallon.

This trouble is persistent and it may be found necessary to remove the turf and the soil beneath, put fresh soil and re-sow.

Cyclamen neapolitanum, delightful miniatures with rosy flowers. Also decorative in spring when their silver-marked green foliage makes a perfect woodland carpet.

September
Week 4

Garden flowers

Label the dahlias carefully and decide which varieties are worth propagating.

Thin the autumn-sown annuals before they get leggy.

Window-boxes and tubs should be planted with bulbs or small ivies and evergreens.

Division of herbaceous plants can begin.

Leave the gladioli in the ground a little longer until the corms are fully developed.

A batch of *Fritillaria meleagris*, the snake's head, planted in the rock garden now will be an early spring attraction.

Indoor plants

House plants will need less water and stimulant from now until the spring. Any re-potting of pot-bound house plants may be carried out immediately, but the majority are best left until the spring.

After watering let the plants dry out before watering again.

Move the plants on the window-sill to the inside of the curtains at night.

Shrubs

Prepare the soil to receive deciduous shrubs.

Prepare beds for planting heather next month (or in November).

Prepare for the roses arriving next month. Have a care when forking the rosebed: beware of surface roots. Hand-weeding is advised. Pick up fallen leaves below the bushes and burn them, afterwards spraying the bush and the ground below it with a double-purpose spray against black spot and mildew. Long whippy growth should be cut back by a third to prevent the bush suffering from wind and root-rock.

Control mildew, particularly on the stems, as best you can, with a reputable fungicide.

Hedges

Give the hedges a last clip.

Prepare for planting deciduous hedges: deep preparation is rewarding.

Greenhouse

Geraniums lifted from the garden should have their top growth cut back to half their length and the roots trimmed. They should then be boxed, their roots covered with 2 ins. of loam (or they can be potted up). They should be kept on the dry side through the winter.

Vegetables

Brassicas should be sprayed against caterpillar and fly.

Cut down the asparagus to ground level when the foliage discolours, and clear the beds of weeds and debris.

Draw the soil up to the brussels sprouts.

The thick-necked onions are poor keepers and should be sent to the kitchen.

Cabbage stumps should be cut up in sections and put on the compost heap, or dried and burnt.

Brussels sprouts, that have not cropped well or showed buttons, may be stimulated by a vegetable fertiliser.

Herbs

Sow parsley for the spring.

Fruit

Hard or ripe wood cuttings of bush fruit, 8–9 ins. long, should be taken now and early next month.

Prune out old wood on peaches and nectarines.

After fruit picking, old canes and growth of blackberries and loganberries should be cut down to ground level and the young growth tied in.

Examine fruit already in store, remembering that pears deteriorate fast.

I am always surprised that more gardeners in the south don't grow the delicious fig. If you live in a warm district and have a sheltered position going begging, I can recommend the slightly tender Brown Turkey, a good cropper, if the roots are kept within bounds, with large yellow-green fruit of considerable sweetness.

Meanwhile, the townsman will find the fig a handsome foliage plant capable of hiding and decorating a grim black wall, while requiring a minimum of root room.

Lawn

Sow your lawn immediately or wait until the spring.

Lift the blades of the mower: grass should be left half an inch long.

Here is a recipe to feed a hungry looking lawn: 3 ozs. complete fish manure, plus 8–16 ozs. compost or peat to the sq. yd.

The Pool

Give the fish a regular protein feed now that nature's supplies are getting scarce. This will enable the fish to build up a store of nourishment before the winter, when in cold weather they cease to feed.

Hibiscus rosa-sinensis that demands the warm and even heat of a greenhouse.

October

Time should be given to getting the soil in good heart for November planting. Get as much digging done as possible before the weather breaks. If the clods are left rough-dug the wind, rain and frost will break them down.

Lime only if necessary. If you have a suspicion that your soil needs correction, send a sample to the County Horticultural Adviser and get his recommendation.

Fallen leaves should be swept up and put in a cage, made of chicken wire netting.

This is the best month for planting hedges. Here are a few of the many:

The dark and distinguished yew, slow in growth: the beech that keeps its russet leaves through winter (a copper beech planted here and there is a colourful addition): the holly, often a slow starter, but with a useful prickly and resistant quality: the escallonia, a decorative sea-side lover, but suitable for mild districts only: the easily pleased laurel or despised privet, both willing and cheap (nine broad-leaved privets to one golden privet makes an attractive hedge, but, alas, a greedy one). The hawthorn, tough and fast-growing, presents a fine boundary: *Berberis stenophylla* is decked with a mass of bright yellow flowers in April and May: rhododendrons are also a grand early-flowering summer hedge for the garden on acid soil: the sweet briar forms a delightful scented fence from 5 to 8 ft., while the floribunda rose, Queen Elizabeth, is my choice for the medium height informal planting.

I am in favour of the tapestry hedge made up of different colourful shrubs seen at that great garden, Hidcote Manor, Chipping Camden, Gloucestershire. A visit to Hidcote is an invaluable experience for any gardener.

There must be no delay in ordering roses, and some of my favourites come to mind. Hybrid teas: Diorama, Ernest H. Morse, Wendy Cussons, Pink Favourite, Gail Borden and Virgo.

Six desirable floribundas: Iceberg, Dearest, Allgold, Queen Elizabeth (in spite of height), Elizabeth of Glamis and City of Leeds.

Harden your heart and dismiss the summer bedding even if it is still giving a little colour. The spring bedders, polyanthus, wallflowers and forget-me-nots must be given time to settle in before winter comes.

Herbaceous subjects can be planted unless on heavy soil, in exposed districts, or difficult town gardens, where it is wiser to wait until the spring.

More attention might be paid to the late-flowering hardy chrysanthemums that hold interest in the garden through October and November.

Heathers can be planted or divided this month. The gardener on peat will find a variety for every month of the year.

The greenhouse must be well-ventilated during the day.

Tender plants, such as the Indian azalea, geranium and solanum, that have enjoyed a summer blow in the garden must now come inside.

Shading should have been removed from the glass: the plants now need all the sun and light they can get.

The greenhouse should be kept as clean as a hospital ward.

A propagation box, a flat box, with bottom removed, covered with glass, placed on the bench, will be found helpful for striking cuttings.

Roots should be stored in boxes in a frost-proof place or in an outdoor clamp.

A damaged root should not be stored, but sent straight to the kitchen pot.

Sites should be prepared for planting fruit this month.

Fruit ready for picking will part willingly from the joint. It may be necessary to pick over a tree several times.

Autumn colour at Wakehurst Place, Nr. Ardingly, Sussex.

October
Week 1

Garden flowers

Hurry up and order plants: nurseries deal with orders strictly in rotation. Prepare beds for newcomers.

The autumn overhaul of the herbaceous border now begins. Large clumps of Michaelmas daisy and other trespassers should be lifted and divided.

The paeony should not be moved, but generously manured. The kniphofia and hemerocaliis are best left undisturbed for a few seasons.

The sooner spring bedders and biennials, forget-me-nots and others, are in place the better.

Before buying wallflowers in bundles make sure they have good roots with a little soil attached: they like firm planting. Polyanthus may resent being planted in the same place every year, so, if possible, find them a different situation this autumn.

Pot up a few of the bedding fibrous begonias: they will go on flowering in the greenhouse or on a sunny window-sill indoors, and serve as stock for cuttings.

Tender plants, such as heliotrope, plumbago and pelargoniums, must be lifted and placed under glass, or brought indoors.

Summer bulbs should be lifted or covered with mulch before the frost comes, because they are rather tender.

Begonia tubers must be lifted, boxed, dried off and stored: bulb planting should be completed as soon as possible, excepting tulips, that can wait until November.

Shrubs

Evergreen planting must be completed before the middle of the month.

Hardwood cuttings can be taken from shrubby plants.

Greenhouse

If in the past year pests have been troublesome, the house should be fumigated with smoke pellets and given a thorough wash down with Jeyes Fluid or a detergent.

When frost threatens, the tender geraniums, fuchsias, chrysanthemums, plumbago, heliotrope, the Indian azalea, solanum (winter cherry), and other plants that have been enjoying a blow in the garden should be hurried in.

Geraniums can be boxed, their roots covered with soil, or planted in pots for the winter. They must be kept in a frost-proof, well-ventilated place in a temperature that does not fall below 4°–7°C. (39°–45°F.). Pot plants are happier left in their containers. Regular watering is not necessary, but the geranium must not be allowed to become desert dry.

Pot on cinerarias and stocks.

Vegetables

Go ahead and clear all crops and dig vacant ground. Pea and bean haulm can go on the compost heap.

Plant out spring cabbage on firm soil, and earth up leeks and celery for the last time.

Cut marrows and hang in nets.

Pick tomatoes and let them finish ripening under cloches or on a sunny window-sill.

Remove discoloured leaves from brassicas.

Rope onions.

Hoe down the weeds between all growing crops.

Fruit

Hardwood cuttings (9–10 ins. long) of gooseberries and black-currants should be taken and inserted 6 ins. deep in a sheltered position outdoors.

Peaches should be sprayed at leaf fall with lime sulphur against leaf curl.

All unwanted runners from strawberries should be removed: recently planted runners must not be allowed to dry out.

Gardeners looking for a new fruit tree should consider the quince that needs little attention and presents pretty pink flowers and lovely yellow pear-shaped fruit, that are such an addition to apple tart. Happy in sun or semi-shade, it is self-fertile, and flowering late usually escapes the frost.

Lawn

This is the time for carrying out final repairs.

Pompon chrysanthemum 'Little Dorrit' may. be planted out in the garden in late May. Stopping and disbudding unnecessary!

October
Week 2

Garden flowers

Sweet peas should be sown now for early flowering. January sowing is often too late for the early flower show. A nicely moist compost of four parts clean top soil, one part leaf-mould or peat, and one part of sharp sand, suits them well, especially if sown in peat blocks.

They can be sown outside where they are to bloom, but sowing in pots is preferable, placing them in a cold frame covered with brown paper, with a layer of sacking over the glass light in sunny weather.

Prepare next year's site so that the ground can consolidate during the winter, double digging 18–24 ins. deep, incorporating old manure and a handful of bonemeal to each square yard with the bottom spit, and adding a generous dressing of rotted manure, also bonemeal and potash, to the top spit.

Success depends on forking the soil down to a fine tilth before planting out, particularly on heavy land.

Note to beginners on planting out spring bedding: when interplanting polyanthus and forget-me-nots with bulbs – the bedders go in first.

Shrubs

Examine all ties and stakes, providing strong support for newcomers against root-rock.

Now that the evergreens are planted, prepare for the deciduous subjects, working manure or compost into the lower spit and mixing peat and bonemeal with the top spit.

Greenhouse

Bring in the first batch of freesias, placing them on a shelf near the roof in a cool greenhouse. Any forcing heat will result in poor stems and flowers. Stake early and support the plant with an encircling tie of raffia.

The cineraria is temperamental and liable to collapse if allowed to go over-dry or soggy, so beware! Extremes of temperature must also be avoided.

Carnations should be staked with special circular wire supports, and should be disbudded, leaving the central terminal bud on each stem.

Bring in the *Primula obconica* from the frame; warning! gardeners with a sensitive skin are often allergic to this plant.

Pot on schizanthus into the next sized pots, when necessary. If allowed to become pot-bound they will suffer a check in growth.

Hardy plants such as the astilbes and Solomon's-Seal, can be potted up for early spring flowering in the greenhouse. *Dicentra spectabilis*, the Lyre Flower, lends itself willingly to this transfer, and a few pots of blue polyanthus will also be found rewarding. Place these plants in a sheltered spot outdoors until January, and then bring them into the greenhouse.

Vegetables

Cloches are a sound investment, prolonging the season of late-sown vegetables. It is surprising the difference their protection makes to lettuces, and dwarf French beans and runners, enabling them to crop on into November.

Watch brassicas for fly and root pests, and spray, or dust or dress at sight of the enemy.

Draw up your plan for next season's crop rotation.

Keep the bonfire going and burn up the debris that may harbour pest and disease.

Fruit

All dead, weak and crossing branches should be cut out from trees and bushes, afterwards painting any wound of over ½ in. with arbrex.

Autumn-fruiting strawberries still look tempting: there are now excellent perpetual fruiting varieties presenting large berries from June to October. A strawberry specialist should be consulted. It is important to buy from a reliable source, virus disease being prevalent in almost all but approved stocks.

I would again recommend June to July-fruiting Grandee for giant size and good flavour. It crops particularly well in its second year.

Inspect fruit in store and dismiss any doubtful apples or pears.

Romneya coulteri, the Californian tree poppy, flowering in late summer. A magnificent plant when happy and established.

October
Week 3

Garden flowers

The dahlia can be lifted a few days after the foliage has been blackened by the frost. But it is not necessary to wait for the foliage to be discoloured before lifting, if the ground is wanted for replanting. Top growth should be cut down to 6–9 ins. above the tuber: the plant should be lifted carefully with a fork and the tubers laid out to drain and dry, stalk downwards, in a frost-proof place.

Ten days later the tubers may be cleaned, cutting away any damaged roots or doubtful looking flesh, afterwards dusting with a mixture of flowers of sulphur and lime.

The tubers should be labelled with tie-ons and stored in boxes lightly covered with peat and placed in a frost-proof shed.

The pick of the hardy chrysanthemums should be cut down, lifted and placed in a frame. The stools will provide cuttings for next season.

Meanwhile, veteran chrysanthemum growers without glass have become skilled in erecting temporary boy scout affairs as winter protection for their outdoor flowering earlies, made of canvas, hessian, or polythene stretched on sticks.

The last batch of bulbs (other than tulips) can be planted: drifts and groups are preferable to regimental lines.

Chinese lanterns may be gathered for flower decoration, and are best hung up to dry.

Find a semi-shady spot, protected from cold spring winds, for the lily of the valley bed, remembering the plant's taste for humus. This lily thrives in a well-drained soil that does not get over-dry.

Ruthlessly dismiss the old and dull worn-out Michaelmas daisies and order some of the modern, almost self-supporting beauties seen in the public parks or garden centres.

Greenhouse

A cluster rose or perhaps a forsythia planted in a tub, plunged in soil in a sheltered place, and brought into the greenhouse when established, is bound to please when spring comes.

Grapes slow to ripen can be hurried along by removing more leaves around the bunches if necessary.

The feeding of chrysanthemums should now stop, as prolonged feeding is apt to lead to flower deformities and decay.

A final batch of viola and pansy cuttings may be taken and inserted in pots in a cold frame, or outdoors in a warm nursery bed.

Vegetables

Cauliflowers should be pricked off and can either be given individual pots or planted direct in a bed in the frame.

Remaining outdoor cucumbers should be cut.

Lift turnips with a fork, taking care not to damage or bruise them. The tops should be twisted off and the roots stored in sand. Gardeners with a taste for turnip tops may leave half the crop in the ground and use the leaves as a vegetable.

Herbs

Cut down all remaining herbs to encourage young growth, lightly covering roots with sieved soil. Kept warm and moist, the plants will soon provide fresh foliage.

Fruit

Grape bunches should be cut as soon as ripe as the berries are liable to rot in a low temperature. Any decaying berries should be immediately removed and the house kept well-ventilated and the temperature steady at 10°C. (50°F.).

Pears go sleepy at the drop of a hat. They must not be stacked but stood tails up.

The last of the apples and pears should be gathered before the weather breaks or a storm tumbles them down. They can be stacked in deep, slatted boxes (up to two or three layers) and keep best in a fairly moist atmosphere. All fruit must be examined regularly from harvesting until wanted.

Lawn

A swish with the besom brush on a dry day will scatter the worm-casts.

If they are numerous, chlordane-based weedkiller should be applied on a mild, humid day.

Clematis tangutica with enchanting deep yellow lantern-shaped flowers, and fascinating feathery seed-heads.

October
Week 4

Garden flowers

Now comes the turn of the tulips, and the gardener is advised to be adventurous in his choice.

There are the exciting viridifloras in unusual colours, with a splash of green on each petal: the elegant lily-flowered, the diverting parrots or dragons, the multi-flowered types with 3–6 flower heads to each stem and the dazzling tulipa species, such as *Fosteriana* scarlet Red Emperor, bright as a guardsman on parade.

The tulip season can start in February if the small, tulip-like, wild crocus, Violet Queen, is entertained.

Gladioli are best lifted this month and dried in the air. The foliage should be cut off an inch above the corm, and later on the weary old corms gently rubbed away and discarded. The clean corms can now be laid in a shallow tray and stored in a frost-proof place at a temperature of 10°C. (50°F.). Cormlets, known as 'spawn' should be kept apart, and usually flower in their second year.

The orderly gardener will be anxious to tidy up the tired looking border. The wisdom of cutting down the brown and withered foliage is debatable and depends on the climate of the district. Northern and exposed gardens benefit from the protection of the dead material against cold winds and frost.

Indoor plants

The amaryllis (hippeastrum) should be at complete rest: repotting is only necessary every second or third year.

All tender subjects, the Indian azalea, Christmas cactus, solanum or winter cherry and other house plants that have enjoyed a summer blow in the garden must now be safely established again inside.

Shrubs

If bad weather prevents the planting of newly-delivered shrubs, undo and stand them in a dry shed, until the weather breaks, covering their roots with sacking or straw, which must be kept damp.

Hedges

Finish all hedge trimming of privet and others, while the growth is sappy and soft. The work is eased if the shear blades are oiled from time to time and this gives the gardener an excuse for taking a little refreshment.

Greenhouse

A light well-ventilated greenhouse. with a day temperature of 13°C. (55°F.), falling 6°C. (10°F.) to 7°C. (45°F.) at night, will suit the majority of plants. Slight ventilation may be given from 10 a.m. to 3 p.m. on sunny days.

Chrysanthemums: stools of 'earlies' that are in a frame should be cleaned up and leaves or branches of doubtful health removed and burnt.

Another batch of perpetual carnations may be rooted.

Gradually cut down the water supply to fuchsias without letting them go dry: treat the cyclamen to fortnightly feeds of weak liquid manure.

Lag the greenhouse pipes.

Vegetables

Tall brussels sprouts in exposed gardens are best staked.

All root crops, other than parsnips, swedes and Jerusalem artichokes, should be lifted and stored.

If there is no place in the house or shed to store roots, an outdoor clamp is the answer (see October summary).

Store potatoes in a dark, well-ventilated frost-proof place, remembering that stored in heat they will begin to grow/sprout.

Lettuce, round-seeded peas and broad beans can be sown under cloches on a site that was manured for the previous crop.

Inspect the onions, particularly the whoppers.

Fruit

Remember: limit the basal shoots of raspberries to 8 canes a plant.

Prune and discipline all wall-trained trees.

Aster 'Carnival' that adds colour to the autumn riot of Michaelmas daisies.

November

Flowers are scarce this month, but the berried trees and shrubs, alight with autumn colour, take their place.

Here, *Acer griseum*, the mahogany paper-bark maple with dazzling red leaves, *Arbutus unedo's* orange fruits, and the gorgeous flame of the liquid-amber, play their part.

If there is a trellis, archway, or wall where the magnificent ornamental vine, *Vitis coignetiae*, can ramble fancy-free, it will provide a blaze of exciting reds. This is a climber, quick and willing to camouflage any grisly structure given a helping hand from the gardener. The lace-like Virginia creeper and its forms give the same dramatic effect and have the advantage of being self-clinging.

All vacant ground should be dug other than that with very light soil, which is often better left until the spring.

The importance of giving the newly planted a good start in life cannot be over-stressed.

The sooner the deciduous trees and shrubs are in place, the better.

Here are some golden rules for planting:

Give the newcomers a generous sized hole so that the roots can be spread out comfortably (unless they naturally form a root-ball).

Prune back any damaged roots.

Three don'ts. Don't plant too deeply. Don't let the roots dry out while waiting to be planted. Don't bury the valuable top soil: it must be returned to the top spit from which it came.

Stake and plant firmly.

Transplanting: there is always a danger in transplanting an old or long established tree or shrub. However, if it has outgrown its allotted space it may have to go.

To minimise the risk of the transplanting, thrust the spade down in a semi-circle round the plant to sever outspread roots. The circle may be completed two weeks later. This treatment, which should be given sometime before moving, will encourage the plant to make fibrous roots before it is lifted some months later.

When lifting, wrap the root-ball in sacking or polythene, keeping as much soil attached to the roots as possible.

The plant must not be allowed at any time to go dry and must be constantly watched for dryness during the following spring.

Hardwood cuttings of red and white currants, certain shrubs and plants can still be taken in November. They should be longer than the soft or half-ripe cuttings. They should be inserted at two-thirds their length in outdoor trenches with a sprinkling of sand at their base.

Ripe nodal cuttings, severed below a joint, and heel cuttings pulled away with a strip of bark from the main stem from which the shoot grows, can also be taken of many decorative shrubs.

Any gardener looking for an elegant addition to the small garden, should consider Young's weeping birch, or even the decorative, common silver birch, known so aptly as the 'Queen of the Woods'.

Meanwhile, if any tree or shrub has been looking hungry recently, it will now benefit from a feed of basic slag, an excellent, cheap, slow-acting fertilizer.

The schizanthus, or poor man's orchid, is an important winter plant for the amateur, and should be given an honoured place close to the greenhouse glass.

Beds should be prepared for next year's brassicas, potatoes and onions.

Globe artichoke crowns will appreciate the protection of compost and wood ash.

All fruit can be planted during open weather and pruning of apples and pears begins this month.

Acers at Winkworth arboretum, Surrey.

November
Week 1

Garden flowers

It is getting late for planting daffodils, *Iris reticulata* and the early bulbs.

Scillas should be planted in the grass and left to naturalise, and the golden aconites introduced into any woodland.

Meanwhile, anemones, either the single-flowered de Caens or double St. Brigids, can go in: left undisturbed they will increase.

Start dividing large clumps of asters (Michaelmas daisies) and large trespassing perennials in the border, but do not disturb the scabious, or pyrethrums until April.

Delphiniums and kniphofia on heavy ground, when ready for division, are best tackled in the spring.

Tubs of agapanthus should be moved under cover, or given protection with sacks or packing.

Indoor plants

Keep the succulents and cacti all but desert dry until the spring.

When the bracts of poinsettias show colour they may be treated to a single feed of liquid manure.

Shrubs

The majority of trees and shrubs can be planted from November to February when the weather is mild and the plants dormant.

Hydrangeas benefit by light winter protection, and in cold districts dead flowers are best left uncut. *Hydrangea paniculata* with cream, pointed trusses of late summer flowers, is an ideal shrub if you are on lime-free soil. The lacecap, 'Blue Wave', with plate-like flower heads is deservedly popular. All members of this family do well in tubs.

This is the favourite month for planting and transplanting roses. Plants introduced now have the opportunity of making roots before the severe weather comes, enabling them to make an early start in the spring.

The newly planted respond to a mulch that conserves moisture at their roots: protection from severe frost is important at this time of the year.

Greenhouse

Partly open the top ventilators for a few hours during the day when the weather is mild, shutting them when very cold or foggy.

A temperature of 12°–15°C. (54°–59°F.) during the day, falling to 7°–8°C. (45°–46°F.) at night, should be the aim.

All glass should be cleaned so that full light is available on dark days.

Sweet peas: remove the growing points of the stems of the autumn sown, just below the second or third pair of leaves. This will encourage a short-jointed bushy plant.

The schizanthus must be moved on to the next-sized larger pot before they become pot-bound, otherwise there will be a check in growth.

Chrysanthemums are vulnerable to damp and mildew. Tweezers should be used for removing petals suffering from damping, due to excessive heat or lack of air. A dusting of flowers of sulphur will help stop the disease spreading.

Christmas-flowering bulbs can be forced discreetly.

Line the greenhouse with polythene to maintain heat and save money.

Vegetables

Sow long pod broad beans and early round dwarf peas.

Prick out the cauliflower seedlings that are under cloches. A widger comes in handy for this work, but have a care not to damage the delicate roots.

Parsnips can be lifted in batches and stored in sand somewhere handy for the cook, but protected from vermin.

Draw up the soil round the leeks to increase the length of blanched stems.

Chicory can be potted up in boxes or pots and forced in the dark in a warm place of 12°–13°C. (54°–55°F.).

Fruit

Start pruning fruit trees and bushes when the leaves have fallen. Beware of being too severe with the knife. Very hard pruning every year may lead to over-vigorous growth. Bramley's seedling is particularly shy of the knife and responds to hard pruning by a poor yield.

If after three to six years apple trees on restricted stocks are growing well, they may be grassed down. Fine grass should be sown: coarse grass is apt to restrict growth too much: if present, it should be cut and left to rot.

Malus 'Golden Hornet'. The white flowers are followed by impressive bright yellow crab apples that remain on the tree until late autumn.

November
Week 2

Garden flowers

A last batch of tulips may be planted provided the soil is not wet or frosty.

Examine the dahlia tubers, and cut away any doubtful flesh, afterwards dusting with flowers of sulphur. If there is any sign of shrivelling the peat covering can be slightly dampened.

A cloche or a plate of glass propped up on wires will protect a precious alpine in the rock garden.

Shrubs

Roses can be pruned any time while they are dormant. Whether to prune towards the end of the year or in the spring is controversial. I prefer to wait until mid-February in the south and to mid-April in the north – when the sap begins to rise. But it should be said that gardeners who prune in December or January often get earlier and perhaps larger blooms than those who prune in the spring.

Whatever the method, strong, whippy growth should be shortened by a third in November to prevent the wind rocking the plants in stormy weather.

Trees, shrubs and roses should be planted as soon as possible after leaf fall. If planting has not been carried out by the middle of December, it is best left until the spring.

Avoid planting in wet or frosty weather. If roots are found to be dry, soak them in a bucket of water. Trickle garden compost in between the roots as you go, and use the soil mark on the shrub's stem as a guide to the correct planting depth. Having trodden down the plant firmly into place, level and loosen the top soil and mulch.

The nursery should be consulted as to the correct planting distance. Very roughly, ornamental trees should be kept 20–25 ft. and upright growers and large shrubs at least 6 ft. apart.

Greenhouse

Don't let the temperature fall below 7°C. (45°F.) at night.

Remove and burn discoloured foliage from chrysanthemums to reduce the spread of eelworm.

Cut the chrysanthemums down as soon as they have flowered and select stock plants for February cuttings.

Discard any plants that have constantly presented malformed flowers: they may be suffering from virus disease.

Order new chrysanthemum varieties as soon as possible to avoid disappointment.

Vegetables

Bastard-trench and manure any plot that has not been dug during the last year.

Asparagus growth should have been cut down, the bed now finally cleaned up, lightly forked, treated to a feed of well-rotted manure, and covered with a skimming of soil from the sides of the bed.

Choose a sheltered space for sowing broad beans and peas: in a cold district broad beans should be sown in preference to peas. Plant the seed 2–4 ins. deep according to whether the soil is heavy or light, on a flat-bottomed drill and cover them with compost and a layer of wood-ash.

Fruit

November is the best month for hard pruning fruit trees. A reputable book on the subject, such as the Royal Horticultural Society's 'Fruit Garden Displayed' is an essential standby for the beginner.

The gardener's aim should be to keep the centre of the tree or bush open, removing all crossing wood in order to let in light and air. Root pruning for stone fruits, cherries and plums, that fail to fruit and other problems, are dealt with in the book recommended.

Pruning of established plums and cherries should consist merely of shortening leading shoots and cutting out crossing wood: this should be done in spring and early summer when the rising sap dries to form a skin or barrier, thus lessening the risk of infection from silver leaf. (See July 2nd week and August 2nd week.)

General

Cover the pool with a small mesh netting to catch the leaves.

Take advantage of dry days to tackle alterations and improvements.

House plants – Draceanas, Begonia Rex, crotons scindapsus and Alocasia sanderiana.

November
Week 3

Garden flowers

Korean chrysanthemums may survive the winter in the border, but they are safer lifted, boxed and placed at the base of a wall, and in severe weather covered with sacking.

Shrubs

Any basal gaps in hawthorn hedges can be made good by bending down and pegging young shoots to fill the empty spaces.

Viburnum fragrans or the hybrid *V. x bodnantense* are my choice for the patient gardener looking for a sweet-scented, winter-flowering shrub: these plants take time to settle down and flower.

Care should be taken when forking, weeding or aerating the rose beds: the fork tines should not penetrate the soil deeper than 2 ins. for fear of damaging surface roots or bulbs, if present.

Heathers can be planted even if in flower: light, peaty soil suits them well.

Greenhouse

The early planted spring bulbs will soon be ready to come indoors from the plunge; first into semi-light, and then gradually into full light.

Paperwhite and Soleil d'Or narcissus are the earliest performers: others may be brought into the light gradually after six or eight weeks in the dark, when they should have made sound root systems.

Once the bulb is making healthy top growth it must not be allowed to dry out, otherwise roots will shrivel, a condition from which they seldom fully recover.

The gardener must watch for any signal of distress such as 'drawing up' through lack of light or excessive heat. Bulbs started off in a good soil mixture will not require feeding.

The support of a light stake may be necessary for the massive hyacinth truss or the wayward daffodil.

Bulbs in bowls for the house should be similarly treated.

The large potted plant, such as forsythia, can now be brought into the greenhouse.

Lights can be lifted or propped up from the frames on a mild day.

It is a mistake to switch off the heat in the greenhouse on a warm day and allow the house to get cold. Far better open the top ventilators and keep the atmosphere moving and buoyant, and you will find it cheaper in the end.

Vegetables

If absent from home for any length of time, beet can be left in the ground covered with a cloche.

Lift and store Jerusalem artichokes and salsify.

Have you ever eaten salsify in a similar way to asparagus? It is good if you like it!

Cut the artichokes down and store them in a frost-proof shed or outdoor clamp.

Parsnips are completely hardy and can be left in the ground, but the long roots are difficult to lift when soil is frozen: a small store under cover, and handy, will be appreciated by the cook.

Horseradish is much in fashion, particularly with fish dishes, but beware of this plant, it can be a frightening trespasser immune to the majority of weed-killers!

Seakale can be lifted and forced in darkness.

Successional sowings can be made of mustard and cress: cress should be sown four days earlier than the mustard.

Rhubarb will force under the staging in the greenhouse.

Heel over the broccoli plants towards the north, and cover their stems in soil.

Fruit

Is another apple tree wanted? I am often asked to name the best cooking apple. Bramley's Seedling is one of my favourites, making a shady garden tree to sit under, while giving a generous crop of fruit.

Blenheim Orange is an alternative and an excellent dual purpose variety either for cooking or dessert: another is Lane's Prince Albert, which is ideal for small gardens.

Fig trees in cold districts grown as wall plants benefit by being thatched with branches of spruce.

Virus-infected or reverted blackcurrants should have been marked for destruction on the bonfire.

General

Gutters and drains on house and greenhouse must be checked after leaf fall and cleared of debris (and birds' nests).

Pernettya mucronata with small white bell flowers followed by colourful autumn berries. A good town window-box or tub plant.

November
Week 4

Garden flowers

Late-delivered herbaceous plants can still be planted when mild.

Indoor plants

Azalea indica is a small shrub that flowers exuberantly in a root-bound pot, where there is little room for earth. The plant must be watered generously, sometimes twice a day, or on occasion plunged in a bucket of water. Rainwater, rather than tap water, should be used when possible for this lime-hater.

The Indian azalea demands even warmth without draught and a humid atmosphere: a hot stuffy room will result in stripping the plant of leaves and shortening its life.

Have a care when watering bulbs in glazed bowls or containers with inadequate drainage holes. After watering allow the surplus water to drain away: never let a plant stand with its feet in water.

May I remind you again to move house plants to the room side of drawn curtains at night in severe weather.

Cyclamen flowers should be picked by giving them a gentle tug away from the corm: if blooms are picked in the ordinary way the snag left may rot back to the corm. Water carefully to the side of the corms.

Pot up the hippeastrums as soon as you get them.

The solanum or winter cherry needs a humid atmosphere, if it is to hold its berries. Weak doses of liquid manure will improve the colour and size of the fruit, if given while developing.

Treat the cyclamen to ten-day doses of liquid manure and remove discoloured foliage. Apply the feed with care to avoid damaging growing stems.

Shrubs

Tread in the newly planted trees, shrubs, plants and cuttings lifted by the frost.

Climbers

Plant all climbers at least a foot away from the wall and several feet away from any tree.

Greenhouse

Fuchsias are about to take a rest, but there are some plants that never become completely dormant in a greenhouse. They will require less to drink but must not be allowed to dry out and should be watered as soon as leaves droop.

Tender plants in a cold house should be plunged in soil to keep the frost from their roots.

Stake winter-flowering begonias.

Prune the plumbago and oleander.

Lilies in pots may be re-potted (dead scales being removed). The pots can be placed in frames until the lilies start to grow, when they should be brought into the greenhouse.

Gloxinia seed can be sown from now until March to flower from May onwards. The seeds are minute and should be sown thinly, pressed into the compost and covered with a sheet of glass. A propagation frame, and a temperature of about 16°C. (61°F.) will hasten germination. The seedlings are best pricked out with a wooden label and the glass replaced over the pan.

Vegetables

Winter lettuce should be covered with cloches.

Suckers from globe artichokes can be removed and planted in frames: I have yet to meet a gardener who has suffered from a glut of artichokes.

Herbs

Plant perennial herbs when the soil and weather are kind.

Mint beds that have been infected with rust should be packed round with straw and the plants burnt down.

Fruit

Remove runners and any out of season flowers from the strawberries.

Newly planted raspberries should be cut down at the time of planting. If the plant is allowed to fruit the first year, it is likely to result in the formation of weak canes.

Grapes should be cut when ripe with a 6–9 in. length of lateral growth that can be inserted in a bottle of soft water.

Other laterals should be cut back to within 2 ins. of a dormant bud on the main spur.

All loose bark should be rubbed off the main rods after which they can be untied and lowered to the ground to prevent sap rising direct to the top of the vine when growth is restarted.

General

See that outdoor stand-pipes are well lagged.

Acer palmatum, the Japanese maple that turns brilliant orange in autumn. The perfect small garden shrub given lime-free soil and protection from severe frost.

December

There is no reason why December should be the bleak, flowerless month it is in many gardens.

There are a number of winter-flowering plants and here the Christmas rose holds pride of place. The sculptured white blooms of *Helleborus niger*, sometimes tinted pink, is a masterpiece, with interesting, hand-like leather leaves.

The plant may be slow to settle down, but given semi-shade, a rich loamy soil that does not dry out, and a taste of manure in the spring, it will respond. The green corsicus, with clusters of dangling cups, the plum and purple *H. atrorubens*, and the Lenten rose hybrids are enchanting, when seen nodding together.

Iris unguicularis (syn. *I. stylosa*) from Algeria is another flower that no garden can afford to be without. I confess its foliage is untidy, but the lavender flowers that hide themselves in the tufts are beautiful. If picked in bud when they appear, resembling tightly rolled umbrellas, they will give a magic performance when brought into the warmth of a room.

This iris should be planted at the base of a sunny wall where it can stay undisturbed: poor soil discourages flowering.

Another must for the winter garden is the climber, *Jasminum nudiflorum*, providing gay yellow sprays during mild spells from autumn to spring. This is a willing grower needing good fare, shelter, and regular tying in.

And finally, please give a thought to the winter heathers. *Erica carnea*, the mountain heath, is low-growing and excellent ground cover. Varieties such as rose-pink King George are smothered in bloom from December to March.

I can recommend *E. carnea*, 'Springwood Pink' and 'Springwood White', of slightly trailing habit, as suitable for furnishing a dull bank, while Celia M. Beale is most desirable being one of the earliest and largest of the whites for its size.

Erica darleyensis is another group growing to 2 ft., and is seldom out of flower from November until the spring.

Fortunately, the majority of winter heathers will tolerate a moderately limey soil provided they are given a diet of damp peat and a place in the sun.

Among the winter-flowering shrubs are the winter cherry, with its white and blush-pink blossom, and a bridal Kate Greenaway look, the torn golden-ribboned witch hazel, and the heavily scented maroon and yellow *Chimonanthus fragrans*, the beloved Winter Sweet.

Garrya elliptica possesses intriguing green-grey catkins, that arrive in February: they are particularly long and decorative in the male form. This shrub thrives on a north or east wall and should be given a sheltered position.

My last suggestion is a small shrub, *Corylopsis spicata*, with fragrant, primrose flowers, not yet grown as often as it deserves.

Three planting months now lie ahead in which to bring colour into the garden for next winter.

Gardeners are often disappointed in the behaviour of their potted spring bulbs. They want to know what has gone wrong. First, did they buy from a reliable source? Was it a bargain offer?

Did they let their bulbs dry out after they had started growing?

Did they bring their bulbs into the light too soon, before the growth was 3 ins. in height, and the bulb head out of the plant's neck? I wonder!

Some lawn enthusiasts give their lawn a last run over this month with the blades high.

Whatever your mowing programme, overhaul and oil your machine before storing it in a dry place for the winter. If it requires repairing, get this done before the spring rush.

116   *Poinsettias: red, pink and cream.*

December
Week 1

Garden flowers

Lift a few of the best of the hardy chrysanthemums in case of a stinging frost: the stools will provide useful cuttings, but wait until the end of the month before taking them.

Label the chrysanthemums, keeping the pinks and reds together and away from the bronze and orange. Labels should be tied to the stool stem.

If there was no opportunity of planting bulbs in October and November, it is worthwhile planting a few tulips or hyacinths for flowering in late spring. But make sure the bulbs are sound.

Indoor plants

Keep your eye on the Indian azalea. Continental plants bought in October are usually pot-bound by now and are thirsty. Once dried out the peat soil is difficult to moisten, and the plant will show its resentment by dropping all its leaves. A soak in the bucket is often beneficial if rainwater is used.

Shrubs

Prune any overhanging branches of trees and shrubs, and paint any serious wounds with arbrex.

Protect tender shrubs with bracken fastened to and through the branches.

Greenhouse

Make sure you have a good supply of horticultural peat for boxing up the last of the chrysanthemums, and general garden work, and see that it is thoroughly moist before being used. It can be left outdoors for this purpose.

Carnations can be increased by cuttings or pipings (shoots slipped out of joint) during the next three months. Shoots of 3–4 ins. can be gently tugged away from the stem with a heel attached.

Geranium cuttings should be kept on the dry side.

Vegetables

When sowing peas and beans bait the mousetrap against hungry mice.

Tidy up the brussels sprouts, removing discoloured leaves to facilitate picking and to let in the light.

Sow onions now if you have your eye on the show bench. They need all the time they can get to mature. Ailsa Craig is still one of the best for the show bench. Robinson's Mammoth strain should also be given a trial.

Protect broccoli curds by bending down a protective leaf.

Potatoes can be set in a pot, box or greenhouse border to provide new potatoes for Easter.

Forcing of rhubarb and seakale can go ahead.

Herbs

Find a warm sunny place for garlic.

Fruit

Pruning should proceed even in frosty weather. Don't be over-severe with the knife and make clean cuts, leaving 7–8 buds on the main branches. After pruning spray with a tar wash on a calm day, wetting every part of the tree and where possible the soil beneath the branches.

Give the vines plenty of ventilation until they break and prune back to well-ripened wood. If pruned immediately after leaves have fallen, the risk of the plant bleeding is reduced.

After pruning, the vine should be treated to a light dressing of rotted manure with a sprinkling of bonemeal and sulphate of potash.

Woodwork in the vinery must be scrubbed, walls white-washed, glass cleaned both sides, and hospital cleanliness observed (prior to any growth movement of the plant).

The best vine for the greenhouse? Black Hamburg (the veteran of veterans is to be seen at Hampton Court) or white grape, Foster's Seedling.

Lawn

Repair work: edgings where the sides of the lawn have been trodden down or have crumbled can usually be built up with a good, sieved compost that should be brushed away in the spring when the grass has made good. Or the worn turf can be cut out, turned round with damaged edge placed inwards, tight against the lawn, to form an immaculate new edge.

Chimonanthus fragrans, a star turn, with sweetly scented pale yellow waxy flowers that have purple centres.

December
Week 2

Garden flowers

Tips may be pinched out from the tops of the wallflowers to encourage sturdiness.

An open, sunny place should be chosen for next year's annuals and preparations made.

All debris from the rock garden should be removed. Alpines are particularly sensitive to dank, fallen leaves.

Mild weather at this time of year suits the slugs, and delphinium crowns are vulnerable. A circle of sharp cinder ashes round the crowns will make travel uncomfortable for the enemy.

Christmas roses should be covered with a sheet of glass supported on wires on a bottomless box in order to keep the blooms clean. Flower arrangers who ask for long stalks may care to place an 8–12 in. high wall of bricks round the plant on which to rest the glass: the lack of light will 'draw' or lengthen the flower stems.

Fuchsias and hydrangeas in containers should be brought into the greenhouse or given protection outside.

Shrubs

Firm up rose cuttings after a spell of frost.

Bays and shrubs in tubs in cold districts should be given protection.

Beds near big trees or shrubs are often starved of nutriment. The hungry spreading roots, searching for food, can be checked by the thrust of a sharp spade to sever them. Larger roots will call for the assistance of an axe.

The severed portion can be left to die away naturally. If suckers should appear they can be dealt with by Brushwood Killer.

Hedges

Complete the planting of deciduous hedges.

Greenhouse

Aim at a minimum night temperature of 7°C. (45°F.) and restrict spraying.

The majority of plants will be 'resting': so, avoid high temperatures and do not flog them with fertilizer.

Begin cutting chrysanthemum blooms for Christmas and leave them deep in a bucket of water for 24 hours before arranging them in vases.

Beginners often make the mistake of bringing their spring bulbs out of the dark too soon: the shoots should be at least 3 ins. tall and the plants brought gradually into the light and warmth.

Inspect the hardy chrysanthemums boxed for the winter in greenhouse, cold frame or outhouse, and be careful not to over-water them. Wet kills more stools than low temperatures. The plants may now be cut down to 3 ins. and treated to a top-dressing of finely sifted loam, peat, and a sprinkling of silver sand.

Vegetables

Root crops should be given ground that was manured for the last crop, and not a plot that has been freshly manured.

A new asparagus bed can be prepared for April planting.

Draw up the soil to the stems of the spring cabbage: this light 'earthing up' will help them stand up to the elements.

Onions and leeks can be sown now in a temperature of about 12°–13°C. (54°–55°F.). Pots should be kept close to the glass and covered with newspaper in severe weather.

Fruit

Examine blackcurrants for big bud. The gall-mite is easily identified by the globular and swollen buds that must be removed and burnt. Heavily infected bushes are better burnt.

The blackcurrant has a long life and is tolerant of most soils provided there is sufficient moisture and the drainage is good. The plants respond to generous manuring and have a liking for cow manure.

Poultry-keepers may use decomposed lawn mowings mixed with decayed chicken manure. A straw mulch will conserve moisture, but on light soils the bushes should be thoroughly watered during drought.

If varieties are carefully chosen, blackcurrants are to be had from June until early August.

Gardeners seeking for unusual fruit might care to try some of the hybrid berries, such as the Boysenberry, with large black-red fruits that turn purple-black when fully mature, the Phenomenalberry, similar to the loganberry, the Worcesterberry that has a look of the gooseberry, the youngberry, a cross between the loganberry and the Texas dewberry, with soft roundish purple-black fruits, and the Zeva Perpetual Fruiting Raspberry that presents berries on young canes from July until November, and is an amenable plant suitable for all soils and gardens, even consenting to grow in a tub.

All fruit trees should be planted as soon as possible.

General

Urgent: check that the stand-pipes are satisfactorily lagged or turn off the water completely.

The large flowered cineraria, a showy greenhouse performer flowering from December to April. Many of the bright coloured blooms are centrally zoned with white.

December
Week 3

Garden flowers

Inspect fuchsias, hydrangeas and geraniums in their winter quarters to see that they do not dry out completely.

Shrubs

Have a care and a heart when cutting the holly for Christmas decorations, and don't rob the shrubs of their natural beauty and habit. Take the branch that won't be missed so that the tree is not disfigured.

Firm up the newcomers after the frosts, and see that the stakes are doing their job.

Tidy up for Christmas, but don't let tidiness be your idol! The self-sown seedling may be a little out of place . . . but let it be.

Greenhouse

There is more going on in the greenhouse this month than outdoors.

Large Exhibition chrysanthemum cuttings are best taken this month, and there is nothing to be gained in taking them earlier.

I am so often asked to give the best times for taking chrysanthemum cuttings that I now give a timetable:—

November. Varieties to produce large specimen plants.

December and January. Large Exhibition varieties.

January and early February. Exhibition Incurved.

Late January and February. Decoratives, Late-flowering Singles and Pompons.

Mid-February and March. Early-flowering (outdoor) varieties.

April and Early May. Decoratives for dwarf pot plants.

Here are a few tips on taking cuttings:

The plants should be in active growth before making a start. If they are still 'resting' give them bottom heat and a good watering to wake them up.

Choose shoots of about 2½–3 ins. of moderate thickness, avoiding the limp, hollow-stemmed or pithy.

Cut just below a node or joint: insert ½ in. deep in small pots or boxes of John Innes Potting Compost No. 1, adding a thin top layer of coarse sand.

After firming up water thoroughly, using a fine rose on the can.

Syringe with tepid water in the mornings when the cuttings show signs of limpness.

Primula obconica should be watered regularly and given a bright position.

Freesias and lachenalias benefit by a weekly dose of fertilizer.

Cinerarias and schizanthus should not be over-watered and must be allowed to come along at their own pace.

The waxy, mealy bugs that bedevil the cyclamen and many greenhouse subjects, can be dismissed with a forceful, soap and nicotine spray, or better still, by painting with a mild methylated spirits mixture. A wound or spotting showing signs of decay should be dusted with flowers of sulphur.

Mushrooms

February and early spring mushrooms are a welcome dish. They can be grown in any dry and well-ventilated building, where an even temperature of between 12° and 17°C. (54° and 63°F.) can be maintained.

Mushrooms can survive lower temperatures, but they slow up the performance of the spawn and a crop seldom develops satisfactorily if the temperature falls to below 8°C. (46°F.).

Winter frames should be covered with matting or straw to keep an even, warm temperature. Stoves and other heaters burning oil or paraffin should not be used, the fumes having a detrimental effect on the mushrooms.

Vegetables

Complete the clearing of the last of the crops, leaving the soil rough.

Start chitting the potatoes, setting them up in trays, placing them in a good light in order to encourage sprouting.

Fruit

Don't forget in the Christmas rush, to inspect the fruit store. Reminder: treat the Christmas tree to a plastic spray to prevent the messy fall of fir needles.

Perpetual flowering carnation 'Arthur Sim', a cheerful 'fancy' bloom with distinct red stripes. An excellent choice for a cool greenhouse.

December
Week 4

Garden flowers

The herbaceous border may be tidied and digging between the plants may continue.

Indoor plants

The 'prepared' hippeastrum, more often known as amaryllis, can now be started into growth. It makes an entertaining house plant, growing at a magical pace.

The modern hybrids are magnificent, bearing huge, funnel-shaped flowers from pink to crimson.

The hippeastrum that has flowered should be gradually dried off and put in a cool place to rest until started into growth again.

This is a star turn that should not be missed.

Shrubs

There is still time to spray roses and the soil with Bordeaux mixture (8 ozs. per 2½ gals. water) at 1 gal. per 7–10 sq. yds. against fungus diseases.

Warnings: use a coarse nozzle on the spray.

Do not spray with Bordeaux mixture in spring or summer, otherwise the leaves will be scorched.

Heavy falls of snow may break branches or spoil the shape of yews, camellias and other treasured plants, and should be gently shaken off.

Tender shrubs can be protected with bracken tied to the branches, or with a sheet of polythene. We usually get the worst weather in January and February.

Compost from the heap can be wheeled to the shrubbery when the ground is frozen hard.

Branches of yellow *Jasmine nudiflorum* brought into a warm room will burst into flower.

Greenhouse

In industrial areas grime should be removed from the glass with a detergent (provided that the gutters do not lead to a water tank, as they often do!).

Conservatory plants should be returned from the house to the greenhouse as soon as the flowers have faded.

If the temperature is high, the floor should be damped early in the day to discourage red spider.

Clean pots and crocks, and scrub the seed boxes when weather outdoors is forbidding.

Sweet peas in frames should be given plenty of ventilation. Watering will not be necessary if the lights are kept off whenever possible, but they must not be allowed to dry out.

Geraniums, cinerarias, primulas and other non-tropical plants are happier in cool rather than hot temperatures. They resent dampness and excessive changes of temperature such as hot days and cold nights.

Side growths from ferns may be removed and potted up individually.

Stop feeding the perpetual flowering carnations for fear of soft growth.

Primulas and lachenalias will benefit from very weak feeds of liquinure.

Vegetables

Rhubarb and seakale lovers can soldier on, forcing plants in relays every three weeks.

Fruit

Complete pruning of fruit trees other than gooseberries and blackcurrants: remove all diseased wood and burn. Sound prunings when sharpened one end are useful in keeping dogs or cats off precious plants or worn turf.

Keep the birds from picking out the gooseberry buds. How? Either by spraying with a solution of alum or the protection of Scaraweb. Some gardeners leave pruning until late in the season in order to encourage buds to develop at a time when the birds have plenty of other food to satisfy them.

Lawn

Attention should be given to adequate drainage.

Chemical applications against moss are a waste of money, if drainage is faulty.

Cut flowers

Now that Christmas is here, cut flowers and gift plants are our common concern.

What can we do to make cut flowers last longer? Cut off a fraction of the stems when the blooms arrive and plunge them deep in water for some hours before arranging them.

Roses, chrysanthemums and lilac benefit by having their stems hammered.

Tulips have an unfortunate way of collapsing: they should be wrapped up in parchment paper at night to keep their stems straight and stiff. Always remove the white portion of the stem ends: tulips only take up water through the green part of the stem.

A tablet of charcoal in the water will keep it clear.

Chrysal powder is particularly helpful in making roses last longer.

Once arranged, top up the container every or every other day with tepid water.

Helleborus niger, the Christmas rose that thrives in a rich moist soil. Lovely for picking and should be protected from mud and rain by cloches.

Postscript

This is the final note of the year.
Of course, you have kept a gardener's diary,
a truthful record of your successes and failures?
May the successes be repeated
and the failures forgotten.

In making this book the author and publishers
have been greatly assisted by two outstanding photographers,
Harry Smith and Valerie Finnis,
who provided all the beautiful photographs
with the exception of the one by Donald Merrett on page 85.

Index

First published in Great Britain in 1973 by Octopus Books Ltd
This edition published in 1984 by Treasure Press,
59 Grosvenor Street, London W1
© 1973 Octopus Books Ltd
ISBN 0 907812 67 8
Printed in Hong Kong